WHATEVER BECAME OF FATHERING?

Its Rise & Fall... & How Parents Can Rebuild It

Michiaki & Hildegard Horie

Translated by
Virginia Larsen

INTERVARSITY PRESS
DOWNERS GROVE, ILLINOIS 60515

Originally published in 1988 as Auf der Suche nach dem verlorenen Vater, ©*1988 R. Brockhaus Verlag, Wuppertal and Zürich, Germany*

English translation ©1993 by InterVarsity Christian Fellowship of the United States of America

InterVarsity Press® is the book-publishing division of InterVarsity Christian Fellowship®, a student movement active on campus at hundreds of universities, colleges and schools of nursing in the United States of America, and a member movement of the International Fellowship of Evangelical Students. For information about local and regional activities, write Public Relations Dept., InterVarsity Christian Fellowship, 6400 Schroeder Rd., P.O. Box 7895, Madison, WI 53707-7895.

All Scripture quotations, unless otherwise indicated, are from the HOLY BIBLE, NEW INTERNATIONAL VERSION®. NIV®. Copyright© 1973, 1978, 1984 by International Bible Society. Used by permission of Zondervan Publishing House. All rights reserved.

Cover photograph: Michael Goss

ISBN 0-8308-1291-1

Printed in the United States of America ∞

Library of Congress Cataloging-in-Publication Data
Horie, Michiaki, 1941-
    [Auf der Suche nach dem verlorenen Vater. English]
    Whatever became of fathering?: its rise and fall—and how
parents can rebuild it/Michiaki Horie and Hildegard Horie:
translated by Virginia Larsen.
      p.   cm.
    Includes bibliographical references.
    ISBN 0-8308-1291-1 (alk. paper)
    1. Fathers.   2. Fatherless family.   I. Horie, Hildegard.
II. Title.
HQ756.H6713   1993
306.874'2—dc20   92-40658
                                         CIP

17	16	15	14	13	12	11	10	9	8	7	6	5	4	3	2	1
06	05	04	03	02	01	00	99	98	97	96	95	94	93			

Introduction ——————————————————— 7

PART I: The Crisis of Fatherlessness ———————— 11

1 Images of Father in Our World —————————— 13

2 Fatherhood Across Cultures ————————————— 25

3 The Father in Western Europe & North America:
A Historical Survey ——————————————— 31

4 Revolt & Emancipation: Attack on the Father Image ——— 43

5 The Cost of Fatherlessness: Loss of Trust ——————— 55

6 Effects of Fatherlessness ——————————————— 63

PART II: A Vision of Fatherhood ——————————— 75

7 Healthy Marriage: Building a Foundation —————— 77

8 The Father as Role Model: Gateway to the World ——— 89

9 The Father as Disciplinarian: Building Self-Control ——— 97

10 The Father as a Man: Sacrificial Strength ——————— 107

11 The Father as Teacher: A Firm but Gentle Guide ——— 115

12 The Father as Priest: Showing the Way to God ———— 125

13 Caring for the Fatherless Child: Single Mothers &
Father Substitutes —————————————————— 135

14 Healing the Father Wound: Returning to Our
Heavenly Father ——————————————————— 143

Notes ——————————————————————————— 153

Introduction

Over the past years, even the past decade, quite a bit has been written about mothers—especially about how our mothers' failures affect us. But until recently not many questions were raised about the importance of fathers.

Our counseling work has led us to begin asking about fathers. We've met young people full of optimism, ready to set aside their own needs and ambitions, if necessary, for the good of others. They have a home—not only a physical home but also an inner home, a sense of security and hope. That security gives them the courage to set goals, and that hope gives them strength to take on difficult challenges.

Then there are the others—the young people who eke out an existence on the fringes of large cities. These young folks come to us wounded, abandoned, without direction, without hope. They are incapable of meeting life's demands; they have no physical or emotional home. So they drift.

What is missing from their lives? And what has to happen if these people are to be empowered with some kind of hope to make life worth the effort?

Every time one of these lost young persons comes to us for counseling, we wonder: Where was your father? And who was he?

The term *fatherless society* has been in circulation for quite some time. But even when a family has a father—on paper at least—is he really a father in the true sense? Does he do what a father is supposed to do?

An advertisement may show a father smiling as he pays the insurance premium that will protect his family in case of sudden loss. He smiles, too, when he and his wife sign loan documents 'to buy a suburban house so that their children can be guaranteed a happy future. But is that as far as his obligation goes? Does it fulfill his responsibility?

Father-Bashing
The word *father* itself evokes a variety of reactions. We've noticed that, for most of the young people we work with, the concept of father carries few positive associations. For them, Father is likely to resemble a raging monster or an empty space. He is the fool, the fall guy, full of jealousy or addicted to alcohol, a tragic figure, a hopeless failure. At best he may evoke pity—never admiration. In such a father figure there is not much to reach out to, almost nothing to stir pride.

This negative father image is almost the norm in contemporary literature and film. Fathers are regarded as a biological necessity but an emotional scourge. As a result, more and more women are choosing artificial insemination without marriage. To them, the father is superfluous.

Psychologists speak of the Oedipal phase, the stage of development in which a little boy wishes to exclude his father in order to forge a close union with his mother. Today we seem to have an Oedipal *society*—a collective father allergy that culminates in patricide. People hate their fathers fiercely, blindly, even beyond death. An expression of this unresolved hatred is found in German writer Peter Härtling's book *The Fathers:* "Even though he's been dead more than thirty years, he is still spoiling my life for me."[1]

Finally we have a scapegoat, someone to blame for our misery, our devastating failures. The father seems not only superfluous but a negative force—an obstacle in the way of healthy personal development.

When a father-hating son becomes a father himself, what image will he communicate to his own children? If he hasn't come to terms with his rage, he can't possibly project a lovable, comforting, admirable father image.

Hatred. Rebellion. Revolt. Resentment. Division. Isn't this the fulfillment of Jesus' prophecy that fathers would betray children, and children would rise up in murderous rebellion against their parents (Mt 10:21)?

The Quest

But people cannot survive without fathers. So it's not surprising that rootless young people who have rejected their father or have never known him yearn for a father substitute. They are looking for security and love. They seek a strong hand they can trust. They want a home where they know they are safe.

They are looking for the lost father.

In their cynicism and dashed hopes, we hear the desperate cry of humankind—the frightened cry of a lost child who cannot bear to be left alone. If the father would step in and reach out his hand, the child would feel safe. Even the father's shadow—a sign of his presence—would be enough to quell the fear.

Fatherhood is not an obsolete, outdated function. Each of us hungers to know and be loved by a father.

What has pushed fathers into the outsider role in modern families? How can fathers rediscover their true place? Is there hope?

We believe there is hope for fathers—hope in the mercy and wisdom of the One who has named himself our heavenly Father. That is why we have written this book.

I

THE CRISIS OF FATHERLESSNESS

1

IMAGES
OF FATHER
IN OUR
WORLD

*T*here is a father crisis in our society. What forms does it take? How has fatherhood been misunderstood and abused? Let's examine some all-too-common patterns and think about how negative father images affect children as they develop.

The Busy Father: "I Don't Have Time"
It's not just the businessman with his calendar full of deadlines; just as often it's the pastor who feels he must squeeze in one more appointment. He sighs, but as he flips open his date book he feels a twinge of pride: the proof of being needed and sought after, being part of the action. What about his family? They'll have to accept the fact that his congregation comes first. After all, isn't he serving God?

The middle manager in a large company finds that his schedule is crowded too. There are meetings for this, meetings for that, time to work out at the Y, an evening out with the guys. Maybe there is a chance to earn some extra money to help buy a new car. Of course, the old one isn't quite paid off yet; but it's already so out of date that he's embarrassed to be seen in it, since his colleagues are all driving newer models, and the young fellow just starting out drives a sports car.

And there sits the head of the company, poring over a stack of documents. The doctor has told him in no uncertain terms to take a few weeks off and get away from it all—unless he wants to have a massive heart attack. So the family will have to get along for a while without Dad. But they learned how to do that a long time ago, so having him gone will actually make little change in their lives.

What about the doctor? He signs up for a special seminar abroad to improve his chances for advancement later on. After all, not only his patients but also his family will benefit at some point—at least when he retires. He uses the term *workaholic* when describing himself, as if it were a medal of honor. Among his peers he boasts, "I haven't seen my kids for weeks. They hardly know what their old man looks like anymore."

Father tries to justify himself: Isn't he the breadwinner? Isn't he trying to make sure his kids will have it better than he did? He didn't have a computer or his own TV as a child—or such a generous allowance to spend on himself. So why aren't his kids proud of him?

The too-busy father is a widespread problem today. His work holds him hostage. And he doesn't know how he can possibly cut back and still meet everyone's expectations. Doesn't he have responsibilities— and for more than just his family?

At work, he has to be able to keep up with the competition. If he got fired, there would be plenty of others eager to take over his job. Then where would his family be? He has to work. The mortgage on the big house is a hungry monster; and then there are taxes, insurance and all the other bills. And he needs to prepare for retirement.

But why did he accept that extra appointment? Why didn't he say no when his colleague invited him to have another cup of coffee? Didn't he remember that he had promised to come home earlier that day?

He says to his wife and children, "I'm doing this for you." But in his heart there is also the secret fear of letting his colleagues or his clients down, of not being popular. He can't really admit this to himself, so he persuades himself that he's acting as he must act.

Back at home, outbursts of frustration are becoming more and more unpleasant. By default, the workaholic's wife has to take on his role as well as her own. She resists and complains. Tension and quarrels become more frequent. She feels neglected and grows resentful. So Mother is emotionally depleted, without strength to deal calmly with the children. She is edgy and irritable; more and more she yells at the kids.

Finally, she gives up and looks for an escape—perhaps a new friendship, maybe a job outside the home. Or she withdraws into depression, unconsciously intending to punish her husband.

Meanwhile, the children are growing up without their father. They too are dissatisfied, and they become rebellious.

Such a family is programmed to splinter. Perhaps there won't be a formal divorce; it may simply be that the husband and wife will no longer have anything to say to each other. They have grown apart emotionally, divided by a wall of resentment. But the real victims are the children; they have nothing to hold onto.

That's how it was with a businessman who came to our office. He was moving toward middle age, hard-working and conscientious. He had spent all his adult life building up his business. Having saved carefully, he had been able to build two houses—one for himself and his wife, the other for his children to use later on.

After twenty-five years of marriage, his wife confronted him with the news that she wanted a divorce. His friend had comforted her during some of the long evenings when her husband wasn't there. With her new lover she'd found what she had longed for: time, attention, a little understanding.

Not only had he lost his wife's affection, but the businessman also discovered that he didn't understand his own children. He had always regarded them as cute little kids, but now he found that they were young adults who had had to make their way without their father. He had been so busy that he hadn't concerned himself about where his children were spending their evenings and with whom. He had worked tirelessly to give them a good future, but had neglected to share the present with them. And when his son moved abroad and his daughter got into trouble because of her heroin addiction, it was too late.

Now he added it all up and realized that he had done everything wrong. He had his two houses and the business, but he was alone.

The Authoritarian Father: "I'm the Boss"

An overbearing father, the one who is convinced that he must constantly impose his will upon his family, cannot create the environment children need to grow up emotionally healthy. Children who are continually intimidated and corrected harshly by a domineering father cannot develop naturally. Either they will grow up spineless and passive or else they will eventually get revenge for the humiliation they have suffered—and this means they'll take their own turn at lording it over others.

I remember a husband and wife who were struggling with their growing sons. The youngest was especially hard to deal with. What horrified his parents the most were his homosexual tendencies.

The father was an irritable, hot-tempered man who yelled at his wife and children for no apparent reason and demanded total obedience. At the office this man was much respected, but at home he played the tyrant. With his wife he was demanding, expecting her to fulfill her duty of satisfying him whenever he chose. He was rigid and arbitrary with his children; when they came to him with a request, his usual response was to say no, without giving reasons.

Among his friends he boasted of his success as a father—a success he attributed to "not sparing the rod." In fact, he often gave such fierce whippings that his wife would intervene in tears, afraid that he might inflict permanent injury. He was quick to punish the smallest infraction. One day the youngest son was caught in a lie, for which he received a swift thrashing and was then locked in the basement without food for a whole day.

This man's aggressive, loveless parenting was demoralizing for the whole family. His wife felt demeaned and became increasingly resentful. As the children grew up, they refused to have anything to do with their father.

The domineering father who expects blind obedience from his children and who tolerates no disagreement will be regarded as an oppressor. In his presence the children feel restricted. His sons will be unable to develop into healthy manhood;[1] as long as they are at home, they will always feel compelled to yield to the father. Every impulse to assert themselves is stifled by a put-down from Father. This explains why sons of authoritarian fathers frequently grow up to be effeminate.

It seems that the effect of autocratic fathers on their daughters is not quite so negative. In fact, many daughters admire their domineering fathers, seeing them as strong and invincible.[2] Yet they, like their brothers, are intimidated. Often they never become independent and end up choosing a husband who will make all their decisions for them.

The Weak Father: "Go Ask Your Mother"

In a family where the father is weak, the mother is usually dominant. Her word is law, her decisions are final. The father is often treated as one of the children, and his opinions, whenever they differ from hers, are brushed aside. To spare himself further humiliation, he goes out of his way to avoid disagreeing with her.

But his suppressed frustration needs to be vented somewhere. To make up for losing face, he demands recognition. Some fathers do so by striving to ally themselves with their children. This alliance is not for the purpose of rising up against the mother—such a revolt would be crushed quickly and effectively, and the new humiliation would be even more painful than the old. Instead, these fathers seek their children's appreciation. Perhaps the child has gone to Mother with a request and has been denied. The child then brings the request to Dad, who secretly complies so as to win the child's gratitude.

Naturally the child finds this convenient, but children are quick to see through adults' subterfuges. Unconsciously, he or she writes off the father as a weakling.

When fathers are weak, children lose their orientation. They don't know how to develop, or which role model to follow. They are at a loss, and eventually they'll likely become hostile and rebellious—not only against their parents but also against society at large. Young people's rebellion is generally an expression of disillusionment with parents who have not been able to meet their innermost needs.

A weak father may seek his children's approval, but he may also begin to abuse them. Here is how it works: He suffers humiliation, and in consequence feels a need to prove his strength—and perhaps to get revenge for his humiliation. Naturally, he can use what strength he has only on those weaker than himself. The most likely candidates are his children. He may abuse them through beating or spanking; or he may resort to sexual abuse.

Some time ago a student came to see me. He was very disturbed. His parents were divorced. According to the student, his mother had always been quite domineering, and his father—who was generally regarded as a good-for-nothing—had never succeeded in standing up to her. She was too strong, and the father was too weak.

With his child, though, he was superior. Here he could impose his will and prove that he was strong—very strong. One night when the child was crying, the father grew so angry that he jumped up and beat the little boy bloody. The boy never cried again from that moment on—but he did not speak either. It was years before he said his first word. This inner hurt had never been healed.

The Incestuous Father: "This Is Our Secret"

Sometimes when a man's wife is not a willing partner, he will turn to his daughter to fulfill his cravings. Such a father may appear on the surface to be quite harmless and good-natured, maybe even religious. No one would ever suspect that he is capable of abusing his daughter sexually.

His daughter may be unhappy and feel that her mother doesn't understand her; she has trouble identifying with Mother. Father and daughter may begin to reinforce each other, forming a secret conspiracy. This bond may lead eventually to physical union—seeking love and warmth through incest. Consciously or not, the daughter may realize: *When I give myself to Father, I receive understanding and warm feelings.*

Of course, it's not only the weak father who may abuse his daughter sexually. Sometimes it's the aggressive, domineering father. Perhaps this man has strong sexual urges, yet he doesn't dare make overtures to other women for fear of being rebuffed. In his own home, however, he considers himself the absolute ruler, and he takes what he wants.

Stepfathers don't have the blood taboo as a powerful deterrent to incest. As the stepdaughter begins to mature, she may become intensely fascinating to her father-by-marriage. If he is not finding fulfillment with his wife at this point, there is a danger that he will seduce the daughter. He overcomes his reticence by acting as if he had a certain right of possession by virtue of the marriage.

A daughter who is sexually abused by her father is miserable through her teen and adult years, and her suffering may last through her whole life. Instinctively she knows that the liaison is not right; so she doesn't tell anyone about it. Besides, the father may threaten terrible punishment if she ever betrays "our secret."

A woman suffering from depression came to see me one day. She felt consuming hatred toward her mother, who had withheld sexual gratification from her husband, so that the father had finally turned to his daughter to meet his needs.

Although the daughter had eventually married and had children of her own, she had never recovered from the inner hurt. She saw herself as a marked woman. With her daughters she was strict and morally severe, keeping a vigilant, suspicious eye on them as well as on her husband. Her deep mistrust lay like a shadow over the whole family.

Sometimes sons are subjected to sexual abuse as well, and it is just as emotionally crippling to them as it is to daughters. Survivors of incest usually find it very difficult to build healthy, intimate relationships with people of the opposite sex.

The Indifferent Father: "Leave Me in Peace"
Another problem father is the indifferent father, the one who simply wants to be left alone. He may provide his family with all sorts of material things, but he withdraws from family life. This father thinks he has a right to "his own thing" and that child-rearing is a woman's job. It's beneath his masculine dignity to interact with his young children.

When this father comes home after work, he quickly hides behind the newspaper or turns on the TV. It's not necessarily that his job is too demanding and he is worn out; instead, he's simply unwilling to overcome his inertia.

It's likely that this man grew up himself in a family without a father, or with a father who avoided any responsibility except bringing home a paycheck. Yet he has forgotten how much he suffered with an anonymous father who was always out of reach.

When the father is physically present but emotionally out of reach, the children feel rejected. Even if they can't put it into words, they feel like unlovable intruders, troublemakers who are robbing their father of his well-earned peace and quiet.

"Dogs and children belong in the kitchen" was the opinion of one father, who believed that his children would automatically turn into useful adults if he just paid for their upkeep and education. When his son eventually took his own life and his daughter's marriage fell apart, he couldn't grasp the fact that he had paved the way for these tragedies.

"But they had everything they needed," he kept insisting.

Yes, they had everything—everything but a father. He had made sure that they could attend prestigious universities, but he never troubled himself to learn what was going on inside them.

Children need their father, for it is through him that they learn how to meet the various demands of life. They need to be able to tell Father their little troubles and disappointments—the playground arguments, the teacher's puzzling reaction to a comment, the unfair punishment, the difficult test, the broken toy. They want to know what Father thinks about it all.

A child would like to be able to say, "My dad is on my side." She needs to know that she is precious. He needs to know, "My dad is there for me. He takes me seriously. He listens to me. He knows what to do."

Children who feel rejected by their father often leave home at an early age; they turn elsewhere to seek what Father didn't give them. And for many this is a dangerous quest. Lacking inner stability, they gravitate toward any group that offers a sense of belonging. They are gullible and easily misled. Many of them rush into sexual relationships that soon end in failure. Since they don't know how to build a warm, healthy relationship, they remain immature.

The Absent Father: An Echoing Silence
Especially in the Western world, more and more families today are incomplete. The number of children growing up fatherless is increasing by the day.

There are different reasons for fathers' absence; we'll look at various reasons in our later discussion of fatherlessness. A deliberate absence—for example, through the father's choice to separate or divorce—is much more difficult for a child to come to terms with than the absence brought by death.

Children who grow up without a father have no way of building a realistic father image. They have no opportunity to identify with a father figure, no way to do the important work of measuring themselves against a father. When they look into the mirror, they see only themselves; they don't know what to make of what they see or what they should try to become.

Such children feel cheated when they compare themselves to other children. Often they feel inferior as well. The more a child is "different," the more disastrous is the effect of an absent father.

When no father is present in the home, it falls to the mother to take his responsibilities as well as her own. She may well be completely overwhelmed by this double role. And when she also has the obligation of meeting the family's financial needs, she is bound to show signs of strain. Not only do her children suffer from the absence of their father, but they also lack a mother who can be fully present and emotionally available.

From this consideration of negative father images we can see that the "father problem" in our society is serious and complex. But what does being a father mean? Can we learn anything from other cultures' definitions of fatherhood? We'll take up this topic in the following chapter.

2
FATHERHOOD ACROSS CULTURES

*W*_{e have just pointed out a number of ways in which the father-child} relationship can be warped and damaged by the father's dysfunctional choices. As a rule, however, fathers don't make their choices as totally independent, detached individuals. They are part of an extended family and a larger society. So in the next few chapters we'll look at fatherhood in a broader social context.

Anthropological Studies

When we look at cultures beyond North America and Western Europe, we find that fatherhood is sometimes defined quite differently from what we are accustomed to. Several anthropologists have researched the father-child relationship very thoroughly in non-industrialized societies, and they've concluded that the father image varies from culture to culture.[1]

For example, the Bushmen of northwestern Botswana, who make their living as hunters and gatherers, have very close, uncomplicated relationships with their children. The father is like a playmate or older friend. When he teaches, his emphasis is on practical knowledge, and he does not use coercion. Because the father does not use force, he is loved by his children rather than feared.

A similar situation was observed among inhabitants of several South Sea islands. These people cultivated small gardens and fished only to meet their own needs. The islander fathers, like the Bushmen, do not suffer from stress. Time pressures are alien to them. Relationships with their children are warm and companionable; the fathers are respected but are not feared or opposed. The children learn from their parents what they need to know and are full-fledged family members from the start.

Some in the West have tried to imitate this style of parenting, but every such experiment is doomed to fail. We cannot impose this model upon the Western world, because conditions here are completely different.

In contrast to the fathering practices among hunting-gathering Bushmen and horticulturalist South Sea islanders, a rigorously feudalistic hierarchy is often found among agrarian peoples, such as the inhabitants of an island in South Korea. This highly developed agrarian culture was strongly dominated by men; women had little say. Women were expected to take care of the small children and prepare food. Besides tending the crops, the husbands were interested only in social matters. Only after his children reached a certain age did he insist on his right to be teacher of his children, especially his sons.

The relationship between these children and fathers was based mostly on fear. The father was more feared than loved, as he often used power to gain compliance.

Among the nomads of the North Arabian desert, fathers have very little contact with their children, so that it is entirely up to the mothers to rear them. When the father—who is considered absolute ruler of his clan—decides to intervene, it's generally in a brutal manner. These children mostly grow up to be quite aggressive. In turn, they become brutal fathers who are much feared by their children.

This brief survey of fathering expectations and practices makes one thing quite clear: the father-child relationship appears to be defined by its social context.

Having looked at some examples of family life within nonindustrialized societies, let's look at three countries in which the Industrial Revolution has changed the forms of family life. In each of these countries, industrialization was imposed very rapidly. The resulting changes were less noticeable in rural areas than in the cities, where ties to clans and villages were on the wane and the foundations of tradition were wobbly.

Fatherhood in Russia

In Old Russia, an agrarian culture, the father was a powerful figure in the family. The czar claimed this fatherly authority for himself—and Stalin later followed in the czarist footsteps by saying, "The State is a family and I am your father."[2]

When the Bolsheviks wrested control of Russia, they found that the principal obstacle to the building of a socialist state was the family. "Give [the people] a bit of family or a bit of love," warned the communist leaders, "and before you know it they'll want property." To strengthen its dominion, then, the new state began to extend its control over the family. Every means of destroying the family was encouraged: alcohol addiction, denunciation, even incest.

The family became the property of the state, which took over the father's position. Under the guise of emancipation, mothers were sent into the workplace; this brought more workers into factories and allowed the state to take control of the children, who could now be reared in state-operated facilities, away from parental influence.[3]

Even after the state was forced to retreat from such complete collectivization, it continued to insist that the family was an organ of the state. The father's job was to rear good citizens and make sure the government's orders were obeyed within the family unit. To ensure that he was faithful to this responsibility, teachers kept check on parental influence through the children. Children and teenagers were immersed in countless state-sponsored activities and programs—a network of control from which there was no escape.

Fatherhood in China
Family life developed similarly in China, where the image of a patriarchal father had been cultivated for centuries. The Chinese character for *father* shows a man with a cane in each hand. A document from the third century B.C. warns that each person "needs the rules of proper conduct and justice"; otherwise there would be "rebellion and disorder."[4]

Children owed their father absolute obedience, and they were expected to approach him with utmost respect. For his part, the father was expected to set a noble example and take good care of the family; family members would then care for him in his old age. Sons were expected to perpetuate the family lineage, so they were seen as links to the ancestors; this meant that fathers reared their sons with special care.

With industrialization came individualism, and young people began demanding greater freedom. The new communist state, founded in 1949, exploited this rebellion for its own purposes—loosening the traditional influence of the family. When the state deposed the father and took over his role, the result was a cultural decline that reached its nadir in the Cultural Revolution of the 1960s. Cultural treasures thousands of years old were destroyed, and age-old traditions were renounced.

The family was now firmly in the hands of the state, which kept watch over every aspect of private life, including birth control. Communes were introduced by force as the alternative to patriarchal families; these communes assumed responsibility for educating the younger generation. Parents' earnings were to benefit the whole commune, rather than their own particular families.

Yet this system gradually came to be questioned. With the abolition of private property, the incentive to produce and to innovate was lost. Today China is dismantling its communal economic system; the government realizes that a bit of private property motivates the individual to work harder. But it remains to be seen how far liberalization will go, and how this will affect family structure.[5]

Fatherhood in Japan

A look at Japan shows how deeply embedded in the collective consciousness is the idea that the father is head of the family, even under conditions of modernization.

The teachings of Confucius, stressing fathers' authority and children's obedience, had a major impact in traditional Japanese society. After Japan underwent industrialization, the father maintained his important position within the family. In this country there was no "cultural revolution." The state was not interested in breaking with tradition; rather, it sought to extract the utmost productivity from each individual.

The father led the way as a model worker, giving long hours to his job. For the most part, child rearing was left up to the mother, who took pains both to pass on the traditions and to prepare the children to take their place in modern society. She taught her daughter patience and encouraged her by personal example to put her own wishes second, after the needs of the community. Meanwhile, sons were trained for high positions in business.

In contemporary Japan, schools place great stress on families; the modern Japanese family has adapted by becoming an academic institution itself. At home, children are drilled to compete academically.

Japan's remarkable industrial development has drawn the father away from the family. The Japanese father is almost completely absorbed by the company he works for. Even after hours he is more likely to socialize with colleagues and coworkers than to engage in activities with his children.

A further pressure on the Japanese family is urbanization and the spread of suburbs, which bring increasing anonymity and social disconnectedness. The Japanese, who for centuries had depended on close interpersonal ties, are now influenced more and more by Western-style individualism. Industrialization itself, rather than state policy, is opening the way for changes in family structure. This can be seen, for example, in the fact that today many Japanese young people are choosing their own marriage partners—something that until just a few years ago was considered unthinkable.

It's clear, then, that economic systems, political systems and cultural ideologies have a great influence on family structure and on how fatherhood is understood and practiced. In chapter three we'll examine how the father's role has shifted along with broader social changes in the Western world.

3

THE FATHER
IN WESTERN EUROPE
& NORTH AMERICA
A Historical Survey

*I*f we are to understand fatherhood in Western culture, we need to go back to our culture's roots. The culture of Western Europe and North America bears the unmistakable stamp of Christian thought, which in turn was shaped by Hebrew tradition. So let's begin with the early Hebrews.

Hebrew Fathers and Children
We can understand the Hebrew people only in the context of their relationship to God, by whom they knew themselves to be called apart and loved with filial love. The history of their rebellion does not change this essential fact, even though they rebelled time and time again.

Although the Hebrews were originally nomadic, wandering from one grazing place to another with their large herds, eventually they settled down and became an agrarian society. As is the case among all agrarian peoples, the father in the old nation of Israel had a special position. He was the monarch, priest and judge within his family.

Children were seen as an undeserved gift from God. Therefore the father's highest duty was to raise up his children in the precepts of God. Part of this duty was to instruct them in the history of their people—a history that showed God's faithfulness. This story was kept alive through ever-renewed retelling, just as God had commanded: "These commandments that I give you today are to be upon your hearts. Impress them on your children. Talk about them when you sit at home and when you walk along the road, when you lie down and when you get up" (Deut 6:6-7).

The father's responsibility was twofold: to implant a consciousness of history in his children's thinking and decision-making, and to teach them faithfulness to God through the continual repetition of the Ten Commandments. The purpose of his teaching was to ensure that his children would place their hope in God and not forget God's mighty deeds. As they followed the divine commandments, they would receive the same blessings as their ancestors before them (Ex 20:12). So the father formed his children's moral value system, setting priorities that placed obedience to God above material wealth.

The children's duty was to honor their parents. This divine commandment carried a promise: prosperity to all who followed it. The child learned all the commandments and laws at first from the father, and only later in school, where study of the Mishna, the Talmud and the traditional prayers were added to the study of the Torah, the book of God's law.

Just as the present can be understood only through a knowledge of the past, the future is predicated on how today is lived. This awareness made child rearing of central importance among the people of Israel; they realized that in nurturing their children they were nurturing their people's future.

In modern Israel, a state founded in 1948, there have been attempts to dissolve the family in favor of a new social order based in the kibbutz.[1] Children were regarded as common property, and women were given the same work responsibilities as men, for the country had to be built up and the soil tilled. Such antifamily ideas were introduced in part by Russian Jewish immigrants, who brought socialist traditions to the new land. Late in the twentieth century, however, there are efforts in Israel to return to the traditional family, where father and mother recover the primary responsibility for their children.

Ancient Greece

A look at ancient Greece shows that here too an agrarian culture flourished, and this naturally influenced family structure.[2] The father was the dominant figure, holding the family together and making all the decisions, down to the smallest detail.

During Greece's so-called Golden Age, the emphasis in Athens was on education and culture, whereas Sparta's culture centered on military training. Spartan youths left the parental home at age seven and moved into military barracks. Of course this took a toll on parental influence. Even so, the father's position was still of great significance in both Sparta and Athens.

Though Plato complained about the wanton behavior of the youth of his day, who arrogantly set themselves above their fathers, the father was generally seen as sovereign in his patriarchal authority. In general, women had a lower position than men. With the exception of a few educated aristocratic women who gained respect within the larger society, women were considered useful mainly for the production of heirs.

When Greek youths entered adulthood, the father's absolute authority came to an end. From then on, a young man was regarded as independent under the law.

The Roman Empire
In Rome, by contrast, the father retained his position as head of the family all his life. As long as the father was alive, the son was legally dependent, even if he held a high office in the government.[3] The father was both materially and morally responsible for his family. He could sell his children as slaves. As head of the house, he had the duty of marrying off his children, but he could also annul marriages. And his authority did not stop with his own children; the Roman father had absolute control over all who belonged to his household, including his daughters-in-law and his sons' children.

Yet during the Punic Wars (264-146 B.C.) the absolute rule of Roman fathers began to weaken. When the men were called away from their families to do battle, family responsibility was transferred to mothers. Many women, especially those of the higher classes, gained a new self-confidence. And when the men returned from war, the women were no longer willing simply to step down from their new role and pay homage to the "lord."

Returning as victors from war, Roman men brought plunder to their families. The general level of affluence increased, and with it the possibilities for seeking pleasure and entertainment. Wealth led to debauchery and finally to sexual perversion and moral decadence. Sexual depravity became common, especially among young people. Homosexuality, prostitution and adultery were so widespread that many men preferred not to marry at all. Eventually more children were aborted than were born, and the population began to shrink.

Yet the Roman state needed men to wage its wars. Finally, in order to salvage the family, it passed laws requiring men to marry or suffer grave penalties.

Polybius, who came to Rome in 168 B.C. as one of a thousand hostages of the Achaic Federation, writes about the decline as a cycle of political revolution in the Roman state, which led "some to greed of gain and unscrupulous moneymaking, others to indulgence in wine and the convivial excess which accompanies it, and others again to the violation of women and the rape of boys."[4]

Yet there were also some who decried Rome's moral decline and endeavored to hold fast to the old ways. Cato the Elder (234-149 B.C.), a statesman and philosopher, taught his children himself rather than entrusting their education to his slaves. He taught his children to throw the spear, swim and ride, and to endure extremes of heat and cold. He did not use fear as an inducement; he was regarded as a gentle, friendly teacher, and his wife and children respected him highly. Later the historian Sallust (87-35 B.C.) cited Cato's insistence that the ancient Romans had built a great republic out of a small city not through the strength of their weapons but by their moral uprightness.[5]

The Spread of Christianity

Soon, however, the influence of the Christian faith began to make itself felt across the declining Roman Empire. The first chapter of Paul's letter to the Romans makes mention of the moral landslide that was taking place in Rome, and the apostle urges the city's Christians not to conform to "the pattern of the world" (Rom 12:2). In several other letters (Ephesians, Colossians and 1 Timothy) Paul called the followers of Jesus to a kind of family life that would distinguish them from the prevailing culture: husbands and wives, parents and children were to treat one another with respect. Children were to honor their parents, and fathers were enjoined not to "exasperate" or "embitter" (Eph 6:4) their children (Eph 6:4; Col 3:21).

When Christianity was introduced as the official state religion of the Roman Empire (A.D. 324), the father's position within the family was reinforced. Even after the empire fell, Christianity continued to flourish, and so did Christian teachings about the family.

Of course it's not possible to carry out a detailed sociological study within the scope of this book; we can only paint in broad strokes. In general, the European peoples were agrarian up until the late Middle Ages. Family life was patriarchal; the father was respected by his family, who saw him as having the final word in all decisions.

As the guilds developed and the merchant class spread, the authority of the father remained intact. The upbringing of children was authoritarian and strict, though usually not brutal. The goal of child rearing was to produce useful adults who would have a respected place in society and carry on the traditions. So patriarchy had a fundamental place in the social order up to the seventeenth and eighteenth centuries.

In the seventeenth century there was a great wave of migrations. In the aftermath of wars and revolutions in Europe, adventurers, opportunists and those who had been persecuted for political and religious beliefs set out to find a home on the newly discovered American continent. They were soon followed by large groups of people, including whole families. The first settlers brought the Christian ethic to America as the foundation for social life.

In the new communities of North America, as in Europe, the father was the unchallenged head of his family. Children were taught to honor their parents so as to place their lives under the blessing of God.

Gradually, however, the father's role began to shift—and the eventual consequences were drastic.

The Industrial Revolution
Up until the Industrial Revolution, life in Europe—and, for the most

part, in America—was centered within the framework of the home. The father worked in the immediate vicinity of his home. Not only was he available to his children, but the children were also included in his work. The sons were his apprentices; he was the one who taught them how to farm or to work with the tools of a trade. It was taken for granted that the sons would pursue his vocation as adults. They worked with the father in order to perpetuate his enterprise. Since each was dependent upon the other, their closeness engendered a mutual trust.

But then industrialization began to change the family picture. The invention of the steam engine by the Englishman James Watt in 1764 was a milestone. An explosion of new discoveries followed. Industrialization spread across both the old and new continents and called men out of their families—for they were needed to run the new heavy machinery. Women took over the households and saw to the rearing of the children.

The growth in industrialization also brought a growth in affluence—and rising expectations. Even though the gap between poor and rich grew larger, the consciousness of having rights was eventually awakened even in the poorest classes. Everyone strove for more possessions and greater wealth, because this alone seemed to promise independence.

In the French Revolution of 1789, the king, who had functioned as France's father figure, was mercilessly executed. People rejoiced in the hope that humankind had "come of age" and the era of emancipation had finally dawned. One monarchy after another was abolished.

The individual's sense of self grew stronger. One's own country began to seem too small; what lay beyond the national borders looked tempting. Colonization promised not only new, untapped sources of raw materials but also new markets for Western products. With the new machines, production had increased so much that new markets were continually needed. So advertising developed to persuade consumers that they really needed new products. A circulatory system of creating demand and satisfying it was developed.

Work became more hectic, and social relationships were now more complicated, harder to define. A system of prestige grew up, and a new morality replaced the old. What one person owned the next person wanted to have. The motto was "Equal opportunity for all!"

One country after another was stricken by this viruslike materialism, until all of the Western world and several Asian countries had come under the infection. Even wars brought with them certain gains, so wars were fomented for the sake of profit.

Emancipation became a cultural concept. The world was like a tinderbox; one could hardly keep abreast of events. One colonial region after another revolted and shook off foreign rule. And various minority groups are still fighting for their rights.

But has the world come of age?

The Family in the Modern World

Industrialization caused fathers to be increasingly alienated from their children. Often the father worked far from home; it was not uncommon for his work to keep him away from home for ten or even twelve hours each day. Sometimes his children didn't even know where their father worked or what he did. Work itself became more and more specialized, requiring very specific knowledge and skills, so that it was nearly impossible for children to become familiar with their father's work and share that part of his life. And the father's long absences placed new burdens on the mother.

As industry developed, farming became less attractive as a way of making a living. People began to leave rural areas. Cities grew larger and more impersonal; small businesses were swallowed up by large corporations.

Only families grew smaller. Large families were less and less common, and ties to extended families were easily broken. The new smaller family existed in isolation in the city. Husbands and fathers gave their lives to industry. The material rewards were often great, but the price was high: the loss of family ties.

As industry became increasingly mechanized and heavy machines were replaced by lighter ones, women began to enter the work force in larger numbers. Women could operate weaving machines, for example, just as well as men. Women were hired for sewing and running telephone switchboards, and huge offices were built to accommodate a fleet of secretaries. With many new jobs to choose from, women found a new self-confidence in the world of industry and business.

As a result of working outside the home, women sensed—and expressed—a greater need for recognition and power. Having gained the capacity for financial independence, they now felt justified in seeking independence from their husbands.

Even children were drawn into factory work, for industry needed everyone. Historians tell us that in England some child workers were so tiny that they were carried to the factories to do their work.

Until that point the concept of childhood was not understood. Children were seen as miniature adults, and as such they were integrated into adults' work processes. Industry devoured them all—and so loosened the family bond.

Weakening the Father's Role

In order to maintain their position as family heads, and also to make up for the lack of appreciation within their families, men tried hard to be successful in their careers. The result, of course, was that they slipped further and further away from their families. Though for a time they still enjoyed a certain authority within their families because of their financial superiority, even this authority weakened as individual family members became more and more independent.

World War II sent a whole generation of men off to the battlefields and brought even more women into the work force. In the 1950s many women in the European and North American middle classes returned home to rear families, but in the 1960s and 1970s the women's movement encouraged women to find their places in the working world.

So mothers sought substitute care-givers for their homes and children. Housekeepers, nannies and day-care centers became popular—but it didn't take long for the disadvantages of such arrangements to become apparent. Even the most sensitive baby sitter could never offer the sense of safety and security that a child's own mother could give.

With the home no longer a refuge, young people became transient. Many moved to the city to try their luck at establishing autonomy. The more money they had at their disposal, the more independent they became—and this independence gave them a sense of superiority. They became adept at criticizing their parents, especially their fathers. After all, the father personified the old system, the old-fashioned way of doing things; and he was never around anyway.

Today's children are conscious of their rights from early on and are determined to enjoy their freedom to the fullest. Marriage has come to be regarded as a temporary commitment; the father seems to have been dismissed, his value discounted. In fact, fathers' and mothers' roles are generally considered to be interchangeable.

But what are the effects on the family when the father rather than the mother stays home to rear the children while the mother works outside to support the family? Do fathers make good mothers? M. Lamb and his team have investigated this question, examining young Swedish families in which the fathers are rearing the small children at home. The researchers' surprising finding was that the mother—in spite of the demands of her career—was still the one who demonstrated the most love and warmth toward the children and related to them naturally with greater affection. No matter how he tried, the father was unable to match this maternal sensitivity.

Social scientists continue to argue about whether traditional parental roles have some innate basis in physiology or whether they are simply ingrained by culture. Since efforts to trade family roles are still somewhat new, the question cannot be answered conclusively. But we would guess (and hope) that this trend, like so many others, will prompt a counter-trend, back toward a stable family in which the father can be father and the mother can be mother.

4

REVOLT &
EMANCIPATION

Attack on the Father Image

T *here is another way of looking at the changes in our concept of father-* hood: considering how Western society has dealt with the scriptural image of God as our Father. The brief historical survey in this chapter is philosophical rather than sociological, yet it will be apparent that the account given in chapter three has important parallels to the loss of our understanding of God's fatherhood. Following this survey we'll consider the feminist movement and youth emancipation movements for the effects they've had on our understanding of fatherhood.

The Dawn of "Enlightenment"
Christianity was elevated as the state religion of the Roman Empire in the fourth century, and Christian thinking and values continued to be influential even after the empire's fall (though Christian ideas

became mixed with pagan thought). The fifteenth and sixteenth centuries gave birth to the Renaissance, a revival of the Greco-Roman ideals of antiquity that paved the way for humanism in Western Europe.

Yet along with a new optimism about human potential came a new despair, brought by the proliferation of warfare. Belief in the innate goodness of human beings was deeply shaken, and the nature of God was no longer taken for granted. People began to ask, "Who is this God who reigns over humanity?"

Some turned from the Bible's depiction of God as Father and instead interpreted God according to Greek philosophy—as an impersonal force, the First Cause and Prime Mover. For them God had to be not *He* but *It*. As the traditional view of God was thrown into question, the notion of obedience to God was gradually abandoned; for, people reasoned, why should a God who could neither love nor hate have control over a person any longer?

This line of thinking, expressed most eloquently by Spinoza in the seventeenth century, became the foundation of a new era which was proudly labeled "modern" and which developed into the Age of Enlightenment. Voltaire (1694-1778) spoke for many when he dared to renounce publicly the power that people called God. For G. W. F. Hegel (1770-1831) the new thinking meant the "liberation of the spirit."

Enlightenment thinkers sought to banish the fatherhood of God from the Western cultural heritage. Reason, the new god, would bring knowledge and prosperity. And, indeed, scientists applied reason to nature and made brilliant discoveries. Human intellect probed hitherto unexplored realms and celebrated its many triumphs.

A Fatherless Humanity

As the nineteenth century progressed, philosophical fashions changed but leading thinkers continued to deny God's personality and power. According to Friedrich Nietzsche (1844-1900), "the whole of mankind have allowed themselves to be deceived." For him, Christianity had been humankind's greatest misfortune.[1] He claimed that God was dead—that is, God was no longer relevant to people's lives. A new "superman"—the man with a "will to power"—had taken his place.

Karl Marx (1818-83) also saw religion as an enslaver, an enemy of humankind. He insisted that the new socialist state would root out religion in order to lead humanity into freedom.

This liberation of humankind became a goal of psychology as well. For Sigmund Freud, religion was a neurotic compulsion from which humans suffered. The God before whom people trembled was actually an invention of the subconscious, a means of coping with inner tensions. The superego, the inner rule-enforcer which hindered a person's free development, teamed up with the father figure and was eventually projected onto God.

So the picture of God that people carry within them today, and against which they struggle desperately, is not the picture of an ideal father but rather a distorted caricature. It isn't the Father of Jesus Christ who elicits feelings of guilt in us and pursues us with threats of punishment. From the depths of our own souls we transfer all the characteristics of a cruel despot to our notion of God, so that we come to be pursued by our own fears—as if God lay in wait for us like a bloodthirsty monster, intent on devouring our hopes and our selves. No wonder we try to free ourselves from this kind of father image.

Albert Einstein, like the Renaissance thinkers, wished to erase all personal features from the concept of God. He called upon teachers of religion to have the inner fortitude "to drop the teaching of a personal God."[2] In the 1960s "God is dead" theology gained more and more adherents, and in 1963 Paul van Buren announced that the word *God* itself was dead.

Filling the Void

But humankind cannot live autonomously. We need a master. So "enlightened" people have turned to the mysterious.

While people publicly pronounce God dead, they are secretly forming lodges. They seek counsel from spirits and demons, and make decisions according to the stars. The New Age movement is really nothing other than an attempt to fill the space that is left empty once God has been banished. For whenever people banish God from their lives, they will create gods for themselves—like the people of Israel, who wanted to trade the God they could neither grasp nor prove for the statue of a bull at the foot of Mt. Sinai.

From the beginning human beings have considered God too restrictive and have wanted to shake loose from him so they could rise to divine greatness themselves. But when Nietzsche's "superman" awakes from his dream, he finds that he has become inhuman. Still, he continues to build up an image of a new, autonomous human being, so that he can finally take leave of the old limitations. In so doing, he continues the revolt against God the Father—and moves farther and farther from his true home.

The Place of Women

We have already mentioned how movements for social liberation have affected our cultural understanding of fatherhood. Now we'll look more closely at the emancipation of women—an important movement that has been part of the reshaping of fatherhood in the West.

It would not be accurate to depict women of earlier centuries only as oppressed. For the most part that is probably true, yet there were always those who played a special role in society.

In ancient Israel, women had a place of honor. Sarah, the wife of the patriarch Abraham, was a highly respected princess. And when we think of women like the prophetess Miriam (Ex 15), Judge Deborah (Judg 4) and Queen Esther, it becomes clear that women indeed had a voice among the people of God.

Even among the Germanic tribes, women were highly regarded. Later in Christianized Europe, women were certainly not kept in subjugation. Toward the end of the Middle Ages, and even more so after the Renaissance, women attained a new sense of importance because of the widespread Madonna worship. A woman was not a slave who submitted to exploitation but was instead mistress of the house and very conscious of her dignity.

A familiar picture of the French Revolution shows a woman marching forth as Venus, bearing the national flag. Even so, such a sense of leadership was experienced by only a few; the majority remained untouched by it. Women have generally played an inferior role in public life. Mostly they were expected to take care of the house and bring up the children.

Women did not gain the vote in the United States until 1920. In West Germany, women did not gain equality under the constitution until 1953. And this equality was not automatic; it still had to be fought for and won in daily life.

The more women advanced to take their place in public life, the more aware they became of their unequal and therefore unjust status. Even when they did "man's work," especially in the factories, women's wages were much lower than men's. A woman was valued as a worker, but as a human being she was not worth as much as a man. And she realized with great bitterness that her worth depended on connection to a man and was not based on her own self. So it was understandable that young girls married as soon as possible to avoid the shame of spinsterhood. Better to marry even a less intelligent man than to be an old maid whose only reward was the pity and secret contempt of others.

Women began to protest their low wages and other forms of discrimination. Why did they have to fight hard for everything that men took for granted?

The increase in educational opportunities has strengthened women's self-confidence. They have realized that they are in no way inferior to men. Even so, women remained barred from certain jobs. A few women here and there succeeded in completing an advanced academic degree, but this did not guarantee them a job in their chosen field. It did not help matters that these women were often not understood or approved of by other women: for the ideal was to stay home as wife and mother or for a single woman to find work as a teacher, a nurse, a secretary or a salesclerk.

Only in recent years have women managed to break into professions hitherto reserved for men. And their success gave them not only greater self-confidence but also the courage to accomplish things that women of earlier times had never dared dream of.

Today we find women in all branches of science and technology. And since most heavy physical work has been taken over by machines, it is often women who run machines, both on the farm and in the city. They design houses and build bridges; the days when a woman was admired only for her figure or her cooking are over for good.

Oppression and Its Fruits

Whenever human beings abandon God's ways, they cause themselves pain and suffering. God created both men and women and charged them to carry out his plan together and manage the rest of the creation. God did not set up the man to be sole ruler, nor was the woman to take the position of subject. Together they were in charge of creation; that was where they were to prove themselves.

The relationship of man to woman was to be governed by love. Wherever one human being exalts self above others, the law of love is transgressed. The domineering person ends up sowing hatred and bitterness, which eventually produces fruit after its kind.

The psychiatrist Alfred Adler (1870-1937) coined the phrase "inferiority complex" to describe a feeling of inferiority that often finds compensation in a demonstration of superiority. This is the mechanism at work in today's feminist movement. Because women felt disadvantaged and oppressed by men, they are now trying to prove their own power with vehemence. Deeply dissatisfied with society, they keep finding support to continue their ardent protest. They want to do away with everything that restricts women in any way.

Many women experience oppression most directly and acutely in the marriage relationship. This union, which God provided for human protection and happiness, can become a curse.

The Battering of Marriage
The institution of marriage has been under feverish attack. Marriage and family are being tossed aside as unwanted burdens, and all kinds of creative arrangements are being substituted.

The revolt against marriage and family is by no means new. Even in the Middle Ages and the Renaissance strident voices had begun calling for marriage reform. And when Mikhail Bakunin (1814-76) set forth his anarchistic agenda in Geneva, one of his demands was the abolition of marriage.[3]

In literature, marriage became a frequent object of ridicule, while free love was idolized—freedom from every tie, from all accountability. The self became an object of worship, and pleasure was touted as the goal of life.

And this is the current state of affairs in most Western societies. The term *freedom* is defined more and more arbitrarily, until it encompasses freedom in regard to one's own body. Abortion has been legalized in the name of freedom—and people ignore the fact that they are thereby robbing fellow human beings of their freedom to be.

Men are seen as the oppressors. One's own husband is regarded as an enemy; indeed, everything male comes to symbolize the enemy, and the slightest provocation draws one into battle. One must become free—from all bonds, from one's father, from one's husband, from all responsibility for a newly forming life.

But is the goal really worth struggling for? Isn't this struggle at bottom the same rebellion against God that we find in the first chapters of the Bible? The serpent's temptation in the Garden of Eden is still echoing in today's world. The superwoman comes forward, with head held high, to push aside the Father-God at last.

God is given feminine names and is hailed enthusiastically as the Mother-Godhead. This movement is not new. The difference is that it is carried on today with new ardor and brought before a wider public, thanks to the sweeping reach of the media.

The chorus of feminist voices grows louder and louder. Zeal has always been contagious; anger stokes anger.

The Crisis: Destructive or Creative?

In spite of everything, the feminist challenge has the potential to bring positive changes. As women come to see their role with new eyes, their husbands are waking up to their responsibilities. There is evidence already of a new trend: the father is returning to the home. As fathers begin taking their role more seriously, their relationships with their wives and children will change. If this is the principal result of women's liberation, then the movement can be hailed as a *creative crisis.*

The alternative is that the challenge will become completely negative and destructive. When the family becomes a battleground, the children suffer the consequences. If that happens, emancipation has lost its way. Then it consists of nothing more than acting out one's most selfish instincts—tearing down others in order to elevate the self.

The Age-Old Rebellion of Youth

When we stand in the midst of a historical development, we can easily lose our view of the whole. Only as we look back does a trend become recognizable as part of a distinct progression, and we can say with the writer of Ecclesiastes: "There is nothing new under the sun" (Eccles 1:9). Yet it seems as if the possibilities for evil—as well as for good—have never been so great or dramatic as they are today. Expanded knowledge and refinements in technology have opened up new potential. Only humankind has remained the same.

Plato (c. 429-347 B.C.) wrote:

The parent falls into the habit of becoming like a child, and the son like the father. The father is afraid of his sons, and they show no reverence or respect for their parents, in order to assert their freedom. Citizens, resident aliens, and strangers from abroad are all on an equal footing. . . . The schoolmaster is afraid of and flatters his pupils. . . . Generally speaking, the young copy their elders, and compete with them in words and deeds, while the elders, anxious not to be thought disagreeable tyrants, imitate the young, accommodating themselves to the young and filling themselves full of wit and bon mots.[4]

Emancipation is part of a process of maturation that repeats itself in every generation. If we look back about a hundred years in Germany, for example, it's easy to see that rebellion against paternal authority was already the basic theme of the intelligentsia of that era.

The Cosmic Round, a group that was active from the end of the nineteenth century through the early years of the twentieth, sought new ways to abolish patriarchal rule. At the same time its members reached out for cosmic powers, elevated the "goddess" and rediscovered early pagan religions, much like today's New Age movement.[5]

Later, when the Wanderbirds flocked together, their purpose was not merely to experience nature but, even more, to escape the confining atmosphere created by their fathers. These young people demanded autonomy and wanted full responsibility for their own lives.[6]

But wasn't that exactly what their fathers had demanded in their youth? Now it was these men's turn to experience the rebellion of their sons, just as they had rebelled against their fathers. Freedom from paternal ties—that was the note that sounded everywhere in Germany.

Then came the decade of the 1920s. The deposed German kaiser, who had represented the nation's father, had found refuge in the Netherlands. The German people were without a leader—alone with their insoluble problems. They were eager to find someone who could infuse them with new hope and reanimate their crushed self-image. Enter Hitler.

Hitler promised to lead the people into freedom; he awakened their sense of pride and inspired the youth with hope for a glorious future. Germans celebrated him as their savior, their idol, so much that his name was incorporated into their daily greetings to each other: "Heil Hitler."

But those who believed that Hitler would free them from the exploitation they had suffered from their fathers were sadly mistaken. Quickly he began to reeducate the youth to make them useful for his purposes. He wanted youth who were "violent, domineering, afraid of nothing, cruel . . . with no hint of weakness or tenderness."[7] As though under a spell, Hitler's youth became murderers.

The bright hope for paradise on earth ended in bitter disappointment. The yearned-for freedom ended abruptly, buried in chaos. The dream of emancipation seemed dead.

The Cycle Continues

Naturally, the students of the 1930s who had hailed Hitler as their salvation eventually grew older and took their turn at fatherhood. The question is, What did they pass on to their children?

Did they keep silent in shame? Or did they try to deny their guilt so that their children could respect them? Their plans and dreams lay broken. For what kind of future should they prepare their children? How could they, who had not mastered their own past, train their children?

It was because of their children that life was still worth living to these men, so they set about to build a better future for the children. They created order out of the rubble of war and began to hoard their earnings for fear of losing everything again. But they were so occupied with their own crushed ambitions and with constructing a future for their children that they didn't notice the children slipping away from them. While they were getting their bearings, their children were becoming the students of the sixties.

So as not to repeat the shame of their fathers, these students renounced everything associated with their parents. They despised all materialistic striving and tried to "opt out" with a new lifestyle. Championing anti-authoritarian ways, they believed they were ushering in a new era.

Young people by the thousands were swept into the counterculture. They made pilgrimages to the holy places of Eastern sects, they banded together in communes, they marched in protest against what they considered oppression. They banded together and boomed their yearning and disappointment over loudspeakers. And a "new" philosophy took shape: the right to pleasure. Everything that brought pleasure was allowed—that was how freedom was interpreted. Student revolts, drug addiction, satanic cults—it was all one big protest.

Freedom can be fruitful only when it is limited. When it is understood as the loosing of all restraints, it becomes a hangman's noose.

The youth of the sixties are now being treated with contempt by *their* children. And the hatred for fathers today is even more withering, more bitter, than the hatred of the sixties generation. Steeped in TV violence, today's youth are afflicted with deep boredom—a lethargy they try to counter with horror shows, which end up dulling what is left of their feelings.

The "emancipated," overindulged youth of today have no moorings, and they are ready to latch onto a new leader. They believe they are fighting for what is right—*just as their fathers did.* They stand up for the preservation of animals and trees but destroy fellow human beings—*just as their fathers did.*

The End of Rebellion

Where are Egypt's great hopes? Where is the shining success of classical Greece? Where is the powerful empire of Rome, or the "Thousand-Year Reich" of the Nazis?

One empire after another falls. And each time, human rebellion rises in a new wave. Its expression varies from one century to the next, from one people and tradition to another, but the basic theme is always the same.

This question confronts us: Will the "emancipation" movements of our day end in disharmony, a chaotic muddle, an inferno that will make the Holocaust look like child's play? Or will it end in a new consciousness of responsibility that is rooted in spiritual renewal?

It is the Father of all who alone can turn people into brothers and sisters.

Will the sons and daughters discover the Father?

5

THE COST OF FATHERLESSNESS

Loss of Trust

*I*n past centuries in the West, families were often deprived of fathers through war; today the culprit is broken marriages. Divorce has become so widespread that it is almost regarded as the norm. More women than ever are bearing children outside of marriage. Stable families have become rare. The throng of fatherless children increases from day to day.

Children of Divorce

"Divorce orphans"—children who have lost their father through divorce—are disoriented, insecure and deeply wounded. They have become directionless, without an emotional home. Not knowing where to go with their pain, many of them are disillusioned and embittered;

some seethe with aggressiveness. They feel betrayed.

A divorce is often preceded by years of strife—conflicts in which the children are more or less included. They have had to experience firsthand how Father and Mother quarreled, blamed each other and were unable to agree. Feeling pulled in both directions, the children don't know which side to take. Sometimes they tend to side with the mother, other times they are more in sympathy with the father. But the child loves both parents.

And now the child is supposed to choose. Which one should she pick? If she chooses Mother, that would mean rejecting her father. If she chooses Father, she would lose her mother. She would much rather keep them both, Mother *and* Father. But she wasn't consulted. Father and Mother have made the decision to go their separate ways.

Was it their right to decide? Did they have a right to divide up their child—simply to tear apart what belonged together? Couldn't they have given it another try? Was there no way but divorce?

The child feels guilty; she blames herself. At the same time, anger at both parents wells up within her. Why couldn't they figure out how to get along?

Perhaps one of the parents has already chosen a new partner. If the new partner has children of his or her own, the situation is even more difficult. The child of the newly divorcing parents fears being supplanted by the stepparent's children. What if her own parent begins to see her as a troublemaker, an intruder, a burden?

There are children who have never forgiven their parents for splitting up. Their lives are colored by resentment and bitterness. They would rather have put up with a marriage full of fighting than lose both parents through divorce. Then there are children who feel guilty, as though it were their fault that their parents couldn't get along. They blame themselves, yet their efforts to patch up the marriage are doomed to failure.

Illegitimacy

Another reason for fatherlessness is out-of-wedlock birth. The illegitimate child may feel discriminated against in many ways because he has no father; in fact, he may feel inferior to others all his life. Acquaintances' friendly questions about his father cause him to panic, to flee into hiding. Every such question reopens the wound, forces a new confrontation with the emptiness at the center of his life.

It isn't uncommon for such a child's mother to wish to deny her mistake; yet the child's very existence continually reminds her of the past. Unconsciously she may treat the child unfairly. She may nag and criticize, especially when the child manifests certain traits of his father. Then her repressed hate is transferred to the hapless child.

Such a situation can become intolerable for the child. Like a prisoner chained to his tormentor, he has no one to turn to for comfort.

Even when the mother sincerely tries to love her child and succeeds to some degree in making him feel accepted, it's still hard for the child to accept his illegitimacy. He would like so much to be part of a family.

When divorce or illegitimacy is the cause of fatherlessness, a wedge can be driven between the children and their mother. Their relationship becomes a battle: the front lines harden, the entrance is barred.

Death of the Father

It's different when the father is taken from the family through death. Even though such a loss is very painful, it often draws the remaining family members closer together. The family has to re-form itself, dividing up the father's responsibilities among the members—providing, of course, that the children are old enough to assume some share of responsibility.

Studies show that the loss of a father through death is easier to come to terms with than loss through divorce.[1] Children of divorce are the ones who most often end up in therapy.

Families out of Balance

A review of studies of children whose parents had divorced showed that a third of these children survived their fatherlessness with no noticeable harm. Another third had to struggle hard to recover from harm caused by the divorce; these children managed to fit in socially, but there was a certain impairment in their ability to adjust. And the last third failed completely—they didn't do well academically, they had problems with sexual identity and they were socially maladjusted.[2]

When researchers investigated the causes of these different reactions, they found that the families in the first group had remained stable and organized despite the loss, whereas in the second group the family suffered some degree of disintegration even though it managed to keep functioning. And mothers of the children in the third group simply fell apart, so that these families were left structureless.

The father has—or at least should have—a regulating function. When he isn't there, the family loses its equilibrium. The result is that the child's ability to trust is deeply shaken. An existential anxiety can develop—anxiety that may accompany the person through life and, in later years, turn into depression.

Depression is the number-one emotional disorder in the Western world today. Social scientists report that one person in seven suffers from a clinical depression that can be traced back to some kind of loss, usually divorce or death—or alienation from a father who worked long hours and was seldom home.

H. B. Biller does not deny a close connection between fatherlessness resulting from divorce or death and later depression with suicidal tendencies.[3] And N. D. Brill and E. H. Listen conclude that children who have lost their father through a separation have a stronger tendency to develop neurotic disorders.[4]

Losses and Perils

When the father is no longer there, a child develops a compulsive hunger for security. He may become quite dependent; like a leech, he fastens himself onto someone who seems stronger. He may also be inordinately shy. Children without fathers may tend toward either a pathological conscientiousness or an underdeveloped conscience. Compulsions may surface.

Children with such conspicuous emotional disorders can easily become scapegoats among their peers. And this merely increases their intense existential anxiety.

When a child between the ages of six and ten becomes fatherless, she will likely first deny the reality of her loss. She develops a defense mechanism that is supposed to "make the happened unhappen." Denying the hard facts, she takes refuge in a fantasy world.

But sooner or later she is confronted with reality. Gradually the truth sinks in, and with it comes deep mourning. It takes a long time for the loss to become part of the child's consciousness.[5]

When a child loses his father through divorce, it often happens that he also loses his home, his neighborhood and his playmates as well. He is forced to give up all that is familiar to find a new home elsewhere. This may increase his aggression toward his mother, because she was not able to keep the father from leaving. At the same time, the child feels guilty, as though he himself had somehow caused the whole miserable situation.

When the child has lost his father through death, he may well feel that he can no longer be a child; it's not uncommon for such a bereaved child to end up with an overdeveloped sense of responsibility. He thinks that he should comfort his mother. As a rule the mother accepts this comfort gladly—and this obligates the child to strive even harder to become a little adult. He wants to assume his father's place—to be strong, give advice, comfort his mother, stand by her. He bends over backward to spare her additional pain and tries everything in his power to restore order in the family.

Children between the ages of nine and twelve who lose a father through divorce react with anger as well as grief. They are angry because the parents were not capable of finding a way to stay together. At this stage, boys in particular may be rebellious and aggressive as a way of venting their anger. They begin to boss their friends around—and perhaps their mother as well. And it's been observed that many of these boys have a difficult time making the transition to manhood.

When children of this age group lose their father through death, they may well feel responsible for the mother and also for their younger siblings. If in addition to losing the father they have a mother who is unable to cope, they are stressed to the limit. If the mother's problem is psychological, the children are going to become "different." They are simply not equipped to handle the loss of their father on the one hand and the mental illness of their mother on the other.

Fatherlessness Among Adolescents
In adolescence, the symbiotic relationship with the mother is not as strong as before. Children are now loosening their ties with home and orienting themselves more toward the outside world. Nevertheless, these youngsters who are no longer children and not yet adults are endangered in a particular way. Their insecurity may propel them into precocious behavior, and they are prone to form intense attachments with members of the opposite sex.

If a girl loses a father when she is very small, she will usually be reticent toward boys later on. She has had no opportunity to learn how to get along with males unless she has brothers at home. If the loss of the father occurs in the later stages of childhood, however, both boys and girls tend to form romantic attachments quite early.

Unable to assess the responsibilities and costs of marriage, many of these young people marry early, before they are really ready to take on the burdens of adulthood. Not surprisingly, these marriages tend to be short-lived.

The Mother's Response

Depending on the mother's personality, it is sometimes very difficult for fatherless children to disengage from their mother and begin lives of their own. Many husbandless mothers cling to their children and end up making them dependent. A mother may regard her children as her source of comfort—a sort of compensation for the loss she has suffered. Her children become her personal possession, part of her private life. (The chapter titled "The Father as Gateway to the World" will deal with this problem in more depth.)

If the child wishes to distance herself from her mother but finds no external source of support, she will remain captive to her mother's emotional needs. And she will instinctively feel threatened. Distrust begins to develop. This lack of trust can affect the formation of the child's deepest self, indelibly marking her character.

Gender-Specific Effects

Clearly, not all children react in the same way to the loss of their father. Boys and girls are not affected in the same way. According to psychological studies, the loss of the father affects boys more profoundly than girls.[6] It seems that boys have a deeper need for a male model than girls do, for a girl identifies most strongly with her mother, whereas a boy models himself upon his father.

On the other hand, there are countless examples of women who have spent their whole lives, even into old age, searching for their lost father. This is more likely to happen if their mother did not provide the security they needed as children.

I am reminded of a woman in her middle years. As a child she was able to see her father only rarely; still, the knowledge that he existed made the whole family feel secure. But one day he failed to come home. This unexpected loss determined the daughter's destiny. The rest of her life centered on a search for him. Always hoping to find her lost father, she gravitated unconsciously toward men much older than herself. And she went from disappointment to disappointment. It took many years for her inner wound to be healed and for her life to be reoriented.

6

EFFECTS
OF
FATHERLESSNESS

*R*esearch *in recent decades has verified time and again how important* fathers are for their children's development. In this chapter we look at the father's role in fostering healthy sexual identification, intellectual development, self-discipline and healthy emancipation.

Influencing Sexual Orientation
When a child is born, it's easy to tell whether it is a boy or a girl. That child's psychological sexual orientation, however, is not yet apparent. The physiological features are all there, but their character will become evident only in the process of maturation. And fathers play a crucial role in that process.

A number of researchers claim that the earliest years of childhood are decisive in determining one's sexuality. Ultimately, then, a person's sex is not determined solely by his or her physical construct but also through psychological influence—how he or she is brought up.

H. B. Biller has found that the father exerts a great influence on the sexual development of his children—especially his sons.[1] If the father is at all involved in caring for his infant, his masculine influence is already detectable during the first year of the child's life. The child becomes aware very early that Father and Mother are separate, different persons. The way the father handles his son, even at this early age, conveys something about masculinity to the little boy.

According to observations made by I. Money and his team of researchers, one's sexual orientation is determined during the first two or three years of life. They maintain that a boy's innate feminine tendency or a girl's inborn tendency toward masculinity can be influenced at this early stage. The longer a child trains in a sexual role, the more difficult it is to change it.[2]

To show how parents can help shape sexual orientation—even reversing preferences that seem innate—we cite here a pilot study done by G. A. Rekers of California.[3] A mother sought counseling for her four-year-old boy, who was showing all the signs of potential homosexuality. The aim of the treatment was to promote the boy's masculinity.

The psychologist remained hidden in order to observe the boy without being noticed. The boy was brought into a room with his mother, where he was surrounded by a wide variety of toys and told he could play with any of them. As soon as the boy selected a doll or another typical girl's toy, his mother was supposed to show her disinterest by becoming engrossed in a book and paying no attention to her son. When he picked up a boy's plaything, however, the psychologist signaled the mother to lay down her book and show interest in her son.

The boy perceived his mother's undivided attention as a reward, and his behavior changed in a matter of weeks. He ended up preferring the more typically boys' toys and games and gradually discovered his identity as a boy. Monitoring his development for about ten years, researchers found that the success of the early therapy was lasting. They concluded that it was possible for boys to find a new masculine identity. A similar study was done with a potentially lesbian girl, and sexual identity proved to be susceptible to external influences in this case as well.

Based on these observations, Rekers came to the conclusion that even a homosexual predisposition can be reconstructed through very specific training, provided that the child is still young enough to be influenced.

Indications of Sexual Confusion

Here are some early signs of homosexual tendencies in boys:

1. He likes to dress like a girl, trying on clothes belonging to his mother or sister.

2. He tries on lipstick and other cosmetics.

3. He is effeminate in body movements—for example, swinging his hips. He carefully observes how women walk, and imitating them becomes a compulsion.

4. He avoids rowdy play, preferring girls' playthings.

5. He prefers the company of girls—to play with, not to sleep with!

6. He speaks in a high voice and chooses conversation topics more typical of girls.

7. In make-believe play, he always takes the female role.

8. When masturbating, he is aroused by articles of women's or girls' clothing.

9. He expresses the wish to be a girl and to have babies.

If these tendencies continue, parents may notice that all this boy's thoughts and pronouncements have a compulsive character, as if he were under a kind of spell.

The symptoms of lesbian tendencies in a girl are parallel to the above list for boys.

1. She wants to dress and perhaps even wear her hair like a boy.
2. She rejects cosmetics and feminine toiletries.
3. She walks like a boy.
4. She refuses to take part in girls' games and prefers rough play with boys.
5. Wishing to be regarded as a boy, she seeks the company of boys exclusively.
6. She speaks in a husky voice and talks about things that typically are of interest only to boys.
7. She chooses a boy's nickname.
8. She is aroused by articles of male clothing during masturbation.
9. She expresses the desire to be a man and to have a penis.

When parents detect such tendencies in their daughter very early on, they can, with empathy and patience, stop homosexuality from developing and guide her in the right direction.

A temporary obscuring of sexual identity is perfectly normal at puberty. Not every girl who becomes a tomboy at that age is a lesbian! The child in a normal time of transition is not compulsive or doggedly insistent, as is the child with a genuine homosexual tendency. So if parents see that their child seems *compulsive* about imitating the opposite sex, they should be on guard to make sure the child abandons this behavior after a time and proceeds in the normal direction again.

It's important that the parents not berate and shame their son by saying things like "You act just like a girl! Real boys don't act that way!" or criticize their daughter with the reproach, "You're just like a boy! What are people going to think of you?" Comments like these may serve to entrench the tendency rather than reverse it, so that the boy ends up behaving more like a girl than ever and the girl assumes more extreme masculine characteristics.

The Father and Sexual Identity

The father, as model, is in the best position to help a boy fit into his gender role. If the father accepts his masculinity, the son will have a positive attitude toward his own manhood. If the father is absent and no substitute model is available, however, the boy may well have trouble coming to terms with his sexuality. It will be hardest if the boy is surrounded by women at home and then has female teachers in school from kindergarten on. (Still, single mothers need not despair; as Rekers's pilot study shows, the mother herself can awaken and foster masculinity in her son.)

Studies done by Biller show that boys who have lost their father before age fourteen exhibit a less masculine sexual orientation than boys who lost their father at a later age. A study done by the researchers G. Jacobsen and R. G. Ryder showed that some men who had become fatherless before the age of twelve had serious marital difficulties. They complained of sexual problems varying from impotence to homosexual tendencies.[4] Other researchers verify these findings and claim that men who grew up in homes with one parent missing separated more often from their marriage partners because of their own emotional immaturity.[5]

A study of potentially homosexual boys ranging in age from three to thirteen ended with sobering findings. According to Rekers, 80 percent of these boys had lost their father before they were five. Two-thirds had, in addition, a mother who was emotionally unstable and had to undergo psychotherapy. Seventy-five percent of the boys with marked homosexual tendencies had neither a biological father nor a father substitute.[6]

So fatherlessness can be seen as a crucial factor in causing homosexuality; for it can be said, based on research findings, that homosexuality represents not only a biological derailment but also failed psychological development.

Fatherlessness and Intellectual Development

Studies have been done on families whose fathers were absent for months and even years at a stretch, because they were on military assignment or sent abroad by their company to oversee a project. Whatever the reason for the father's absence, children reacted negatively to the separation. The earlier the child experiences a separation, the greater is the damage suffered.[7] Simply put, children need their fathers to be *present*.

Many parents think that a small child is still too young to even register the separation. But that is not so. A child's world includes both Father and Mother. Very early on, the child develops a bond with both. If, suddenly, the father is no longer there, the child's world breaks apart. He feels lost. He is no longer free to embrace his surroundings spontaneously and take in all that is new. The inner drive to conquer his world loses its intensity.

Regression in development is a typical sign of grief or mourning. The child develops in reverse, as it were. Even an infant reacts negatively to the father's absence. She becomes lethargic, showing no interest in play, and her motor development slows down. As a result, she has a hard time adapting socially as well.

A child's intellectual capability is challenged by interaction with his father. The child finds his father's presence stimulating. This has a particular influence on the child's mathematical ability, as men tend to solve problems in an analytical fashion.[8] Even though today there is an emphasis on training girls in analytical thinking, fathers still seem to tackle problems more objectively than mothers. Women are often guided more by their intuition (which we recognize as another valuable way of knowing), whereas men prefer objective analysis. Thus the father can be a sort of orientation map for the child's problem solving, helping the child to examine a matter objectively. This objectivity promotes mathematical thinking.

Fatherlessness and Self-Discipline

The lack of moral self-control is a great problem today. In this area, too, the father plays a crucial role.

The studies of W. Mischel show that many fatherless children want to have their needs satisfied immediately.[9] They are not in the habit of postponing their desires. These children have not learned to defer their own demands, to deal with the fact that some wishes cannot be fulfilled right away—and some may never be fulfilled. Fatherless children tend to be demanding and expect those around them to grant their desires right away. They simply take what they want.

A little experiment proved this point. Treats were promised to a group of children. The children were allowed to determine when the treats should be passed out. If they wanted them right away, they would get only a small amount; if they were willing to wait a week, however, they would get twice as much. The majority of the children who had grown up fatherless preferred to receive their share immediately.[10] And children of divorced parents had a harder time sticking to the decision to postpone gratification of their need than did children whose fathers had died. Apparently these children of divorce had somehow gotten the idea that they had been short-changed in life, deprived of something that they needed to make up for right away.

Children who can identify positively with their father have higher moral standards than children who had no male role model or whose idea of a father was negative.[11] In our therapeutic practice, we've often seen that clients who have difficulty keeping appointments have a hard time with self-discipline in general. And research shows that this is connected to fatherlessness: J. A. M. Meerloo confirms that the majority of psychotherapy clients who have trouble with self-discipline grew up fatherless or else had problems relating to their fathers.[12]

The most serious manifestation of this link is the high proportion of juvenile criminals who are fatherless. And a close connection seems to exist between the current increase in divorce and the increase in crime.

Healthy Emancipation

Emancipation, which means "release," is a human effort to escape from a position of dependency. This striving is an innate drive that can be observed in small children.

The struggle for emancipation is initially good, even necessary for a person to become mature and independent. From an early age, children begin refusing adult help, wishing to "do it myself!" Each positive experience strengthens their self-confidence and gives them courage to take on greater challenges.

When children are infantilized—forced to remain helpless while adults do every single thing for them—they will never develop their own strengths. They will grow up dissatisfied and unhappy.

Since a child is not able to live autonomously, however, liberation can never be absolute. So parents need to create some free space in which their children can develop and test their own strengths and abilities, but at the same time enjoy safety and security. Children cannot develop in total freedom. They orient themselves in relation to limits—and the father's role in setting limits is critically important.

A Toxic Freedom

When the urge for freedom is elevated into the highest good, it comes to resemble a dangerous chemical substance that causes nothing but destruction. It's like splitting atoms. As long as the atoms are embedded in the system, they have a constructive, creative function— they generate energy that can be harnessed. But set free and split, they are deadly. In the same way the family needs to provide the essential structure for the child's healthy development.

A child lives in oneness with Father and Mother. When the structure of safety is in place, the child's world is bright and trustworthy. But when no limits are maintained, there is no security.

For example, children who are fed televised images of cruelty and perversion are not being properly protected. They are not equipped to handle adult fare. Inside they become homeless, for home is not a refuge from the world's evil.

It is a sign of maturity when a person begins to think critically and independently. But young children should not be presented with adult problems and expected to think critically. They are in the process of gaining a foundation for their lives, and too-early exposure to adult problems undermines that crucial foundation.

In the current drive to enlighten children at an early age, every veil is being lifted, and the young are being left with no self-protection, no modesty. Without modesty, sex becomes prostitution and chastity becomes a marketable commodity that can be exchanged again and again.

If the boundaries set by fathers are declared out of date and ignored, the child loses the firm structure that can keep life from falling apart. When children are urged to set aside traditional standards before they have even had a chance to test them, they come to believe that their rights are virtually infinite, stretching across the boundaries that separate individuals. Thus everything that brings pleasure is good, and everyone—the government, the church, society at large—is there to serve the individual and to pay in advance for his or her future. The person becomes a greedy consumer, devouring everything within reach and seeking risky adventures to provide ever-new thrills.

Freedom without boundaries destabilizes the inner being.

The Foundation of Community
Emancipation does not lead to community, for it creates egocentric individuals who, though they may join the mob, still cherish the goal

of self-realization. And that means isolation.

The foundation of community is *renunciation*. Members of a healthy family or community take each other into consideration. One's own well-being is dependent upon the well-being of one's neighbor. The motto is not "You for me" but "Me for you." That is love.

Emancipation without love is a curse that contains the germ of self-destruction. Its source is Satan, who takes and twists the good things God has made. Where God calls for love, Satan substitutes egocentrism.

As long as one lives with a focus on self, one cannot possibly function in community. Such a life leads to anarchy and finally to self-destruction and death. And that is Satan's ultimate goal: total annihilation.

Where love is cheapened to mere sexuality, without tenderness, self-denial or responsibility, a person is robbed of the most beautiful experience possible: the happiness of mutual self-giving.

The Family and the State

History has taught us that a demoralized people cannot survive. Without the inner structure that can lead them to responsible choices, they slip easily into the clutches of tyrants.

Moral principles are like a backbone that prevent a person—and a community—from collapsing. That is why morals must be fortified.

And that is why the community and the nation need the family. The state cannot replace the family. Only the family can provide the structure of love and limits that can produce well-balanced, responsible citizens.

Training for taking one's place in the larger community has to take place at the very core of life—in the family. It is parents who can teach a child to respect the lives of others. He can be guided toward kindness and helpfulness; she can learn to offer the community her particular gifts and abilities. He can learn to give rather than to demand. She can learn to respect her neighbor as her equal, even when the neighbor has a different skin color or does things differently. All of these attitudes are fostered first of all in the home.

Fruitful Freedom

This sense of responsibility can develop only when a person acknowledges God as Creator and Father. And it is this inner commitment, paradoxically, that makes a person free.

God has given us life, but the gift of life makes sense and can develop only in dependence. That's why emancipation without commitment to the Father cannot succeed.

Real freedom is quite different from the quest for emancipation for its own sake. Real freedom does not mean that one is free to do evil or to follow one's basest instincts, but rather that one is free to serve one's neighbor in obedience to God. Such freedom is not dependent on external circumstances or conditions. It is rooted in love.

A Call to Fathers

A recent study of German couples who became parents in the 1970s yielded an interesting finding. These parents, many of whom had rejected marriage and religion for themselves and spoke scornfully of the Protestant work ethic, nevertheless wished to instill these traditional values in their own children. The fathers in the survey particularly valued achievement, competition and self-discipline in their children.[13]

Though society appeared—and still appears—to be on the brink of dissolving all previously cherished values, many hunger to rediscover those lost values. And in the past fifteen years or so the longing for a father has reawakened, especially in the technologically advanced nations of North America and Western Europe.

The father is making a comeback. He is seen in courses on infant care, and he even shows up at classes for expectant mothers so that he can be in the delivery room when his baby is born. He can be seen strolling with a baby perched on his back, or squatting in the sandbox with his son or daughter. He pushes the grocery cart through the supermarket and takes his child to school.

Fathers are popular again. But many of them need to learn what it really means to be a father. And many of them still don't understand how very important they are to their children's well-being.

Fathers Are Essential

The evidence is in, and it is indisputable: Fathers are essential. In fact, our society is in danger of collapsing for want of strong, loving fathers.

Can Christian families make a difference amid the crisis of father-lessness? Can we empower fathers to take up their role with confidence, in the power of the Spirit? Can we begin to rebuild a positive vision of fatherhood?

The answer to all these questions is yes. The chapters that follow will offer a vision of holy, empowered fatherhood—and practical suggestions for living out the vision.

II

A VISION OF
FATHERHOOD

7

HEALTHY MARRIAGE

Building a Foundation

*W*hat can a man do to be the kind of father his children need? What kinds of things are expected of him, and how can he fulfill those expectations?

The basic requirement for influencing children positively is a solid marriage. That is the foundation for child rearing.

If family life is to allow each member to thrive, the father and mother's marriage must be intact. The relationship between child and parents is founded on the oneness between mother and father. And the husband and wife must both take responsibility for nurturing the relationship between them.

Many people come to our center seeking help to mend a broken marriage. But what good does it do to speak with one marriage partner when the other has abdicated his or her share of the responsibility? Husband and wife must invest equally if the marriage is to work. That seems obvious, but in daily life it's all too common for one spouse to lay both the responsibility and the blame for everything on the other. Let's look at the key ingredients of a healthy marriage.

Love and Commitment

Basic to a good marriage is *love*, the quiet, supportive certainty that one is there for the other. This love isn't necessarily based on a feeling. To love is primarily to respect and cherish the other.

If someone is of value to me, then I am prepared to pay a price for our relationship. This price is exclusivity, which means that I cannot exchange or replace my partner. The relationship we share is unique.

So many people today enter marriage with the secret thought that if it doesn't go the way I had hoped, I can get out anytime. Or rather than run the risk of failing at marriage, many simply opt for living together, no strings attached. This sort of relationship, however, does not express love; it is actually a selfish exploitation of the other person. Real love provides security, with fidelity as its seal.

Whoever enters a marriage with the idea that it may be temporary has already betrayed it. For a marriage requires loyalty—no matter how disillusioned one partner may become with the other, no matter what dire misfortunes may seem to make staying together impossible. Not until I am sure of my partner can I open myself up to him.

Faithfulness, then, is the foundation on which trust develops. And this trust must be mutual. Love without trust is not love at all; it is a business transaction. All too often relationships between men and women are actually based on nothing but the mutual satisfaction of needs. When I use another person to meet my own need for love, or to satisfy my own desires, I dishonor her. This is not what marriage is all about.

When a woman perceives that her husband desires her body but is not willing to treat her as a whole person, she feels cheapened and degraded. Similarly, when a wife tries to control her husband by refusing to give herself to him, she is using her sexuality as a means to a selfish end. In a sexual union the two partners must be of one accord. Only when they are in harmony can their sexuality bring joy to both.

It is easy for love to be reduced to mere satisfaction of desire, an experience that requires ever-new techniques. Sexuality is detached from its deeper meaning when a couple decides from the start that they are unwilling to have a child, the fruit of love. We are convinced that a couple that has opted for an abortion can never again enjoy marital sex to its fullest. The guilt of selfishness and violence becomes a burden on the marriage, so that there is no room for joy. Confused with lust, delight is lost.

But when love reaches fruition in conception, it reaches out toward a new and solemn responsibility. And this shared responsibility links the two new parents together on the deepest level. Countless parents will testify that the shared joy of conceiving a child has bound them to each other to a degree that they had never before experienced.

Communication

But there is another element that is crucial to the success of a marriage: communication.

There are couples who have been married for twenty or thirty years and seem to have nothing more to say to each other. They are like a spring that has dried up. When we look closer, we find that they never really did talk to each other. Instead, each one went around and around the track of a personal monologue.

Such couples don't understand that talking with each other is more than just conveying or exchanging information. Sometimes the hours spent together yield dialogue that would read like a telegram—brief, curt, to the point. Television has replaced conversation, so that the individual is reduced to silence. There is need to talk only to accomplish the day-to-day business of living.

Here is another common pattern of miscommunication in marriage. The husband comes home from work exhausted and is greeted by an unbroken torrent of speech from his wife, who reports all the bad things the children have done and carries on about the failings and faults of the neighbors.

Or the wife must listen as the husband describes the delightful qualities of other women and compares her to his colleague's charming spouse. The wife gets the impression that she is not good enough to engage her husband's attention. This hurts her and leaves a dangerous residue of bitterness. And this, again, is not communication.

Good communication is made up of two critical elements: truth and love. Communication that springs out of truth and love is bound to succeed. And the good news is that this kind of communication can be learned! We have discovered again and again that even seemingly hopeless marital conflicts can be resolved through improved communication—though the solution comes only when each partner is willing to change instead of waiting for the other one to change.

The two partners are equally accountable for good communication. In explaining this to couples we often speak of an *exchange*—that is, I give what I have and receive what the other person gives me. When this exchange takes place in truth and love, then what I receive will build me up and what I give will be of service to my partner.

Affirmation

One husband and wife considered their differences irreconcilable. The wife was always right. Every time the husband, in his clumsy way, began to express an opinion, she swiftly flattened him with contradictions so that he never got a chance to present his view fully. At first he had tried to clear up misunderstandings, but eventually he had given up. He just couldn't get a fair hearing from his wife, and he was no match for her.

The wife was domineering, always sure that she knew what her husband wanted to say. Even in the presence of other people she anticipated what he was about to say and either said it for him or challenged it. Such behavior was quite humiliating for the man, and he was left in a bad mood for days after one of these embarrassing incidents. So whenever possible he avoided being with his wife in public.

Each of them barely tolerated the other. Of course, the husband couldn't get a word in edgewise to explain to his wife how he felt about her treatment of him. And not surprisingly, he had long since ceased desiring her as a woman. After a time he spent as little time at home as possible. He buried himself in his work at the office and became quite skilled at finding excuses to put off going home.

The wife was not at all pleased with his use of time, and she let him know it. Scarcely would he have one foot in the door at home than she would launch her attack, scalding him with fierce reproaches and verbal abuse. And wishing not to appear spineless in front of the children, he yelled back. This was their daily welcome-home ritual.

The effect on the children is not hard to guess: soon they, too, were screaming at each other and spoke insolently to their parents. The parents couldn't stand this, so they slapped the children around to teach them some manners. The family's life quickly degenerated into chaos.

On the brink of divorce, this couple came to us. The wife was firmly convinced that it was up to the husband to change. For his part, the husband insisted that his wife was to blame for their problems. Yet since they wished to delay a divorce for the sake of the children, they agreed to give their marriage one more chance.

We started out by working systematically on communication; to my great relief, both of them agreed to the new pattern I suggested. First of all, the wife had to learn to let her husband have his full say, without interrupting him with her interpretation of his ideas. The husband, at the same time, had to learn to verbalize his thoughts and feelings. The wife was allowed to express her view only when her husband had finished expressing his. And she was not allowed to be aggressive; she had to speak with careful neutrality.

On this neutral plane, they began to listen to each other. The more she listened, the more courageous he became. Each of them began, too, to let the other person's opinion stand even when they did not agree.

We proceeded step by step in this fashion, and in each counseling session they were asked to relate their experiences. And they learned—both of them. One learned to listen, the other to talk. They began to rediscover each other, and that renewed their courage. Then they learned to put their new positive feelings into words.

Each learned to affirm the other, to give credit without cutting down in the next breath. They learned to take one another's comments in a positive light, and to comment on each other's good qualities. Through this kind of affirmation they strengthened each other's feelings of self-worth. The result was gratitude and a sense of release. They developed a new openness, a readiness to accept the other without conditions.

The nightly reproaches stopped. The husband began coming home from the office earlier. He even caught himself looking forward to coming home to his family.

Of course, the children noticed their parents' changed behavior. The daily tensions and quarrels became rarer, and the children even heard the parents laughing together from time to time. The children's aggressiveness subsided.

Today this family is on the road to emotional recovery because the husband and wife learned one invaluable lesson: to talk *to* each other rather than *at* each other.

Honesty and Harmony

A good marriage is marked by openness and candor. Neither partner keeps secrets from the other. Husband and wife are able to tell each other the truth without causing needless pain—because love underlies everything. They aren't evasive but are ready to answer questions, even when the truth may be unpleasant.

Here are a few other ingredients of a healthy marriage. There is no patronizing or condescension. Neither partner uses the other as a means of showing off. The relationship is free from jealousy. The husband and wife agree on how their children are to be brought up. And one will never blame or criticize the other in front of the children.

In a happy marriage, each partner is content in his or her sexual identity: the man as man and the woman as woman. It's all too common today that sex roles are shifting and ill-defined. Then the man does not know how to be husband and father, while the woman isn't satisfied with her femininity and so cannot enter fully into her function of mothering. In a wholesome marriage the two partners complement each other.

A solid marriage is vital to wise, loving parenting. When parents are happy in their marriage, their children will be happy as well.

When Life Begins

Research has verified that a fetus can be influenced in its mother's womb. Even though its nervous system is separate from the mother's, a hormonal connection exists between the two. The fetus perceives both negative and positive reactions within the mother. Since depression and fear stimulate the flow of adrenaline into the bloodstream, anything that upsets the mother is bound to affect the unborn child. Joyful excitement will be communicated to the child as well. And the mother's regular heartbeat, along with the rhythmic movements of her gait, is calming to the child within.

Even before the child is born, the father can influence his child indirectly. When he supports his wife and does what he can to make the months of pregnancy as free of stress as possible, he is influencing the life of his child in a positive way.

As husband and wife prepare together for the child's arrival, their shared concerns bind them closer together and assure the child of a warm welcome. There are a hundred little decisions to make when it comes to getting things ready for the baby. The husband can accompany his wife to purchase what the little one will need. He should help her decide and plan.

When the husband is actively involved in this time of preparation, he develops a greater sense of responsibility. Birth and infant care are no longer regarded as a woman's job and left entirely to the mother. His participation helps her to feel supported and loved.

The Wonder of Birth

It has been shown time and again that the husband's presence during the hardest part of a baby's delivery is of invaluable help to the wife. And for the husband, this experience signifies a deepening of the bond between them. He becomes involved in the painful process of birthing and witnesses the beginning of a new life. By his presence at the birth he communicates to his wife, "You are not alone. We bear things together. This is *our* child." As he watches the child emerge, and perhaps helps with its immediate care, he gains a very special feeling for his new son or daughter.

Numerous studies have confirmed that a natural birth is still the best for the mother-child relationship. It would appear that the bond between the mother and a child born by caesarean section is not as deep. Evidently the pains borne by the mother during natural childbirth serve to strengthen the tie. And it's interesting that fathers report similar reactions. A father who assists his wife during delivery has a stronger tie to his child than does the father who just waits on the other side of the door. A father who helps in childbirth is also more likely to help care for the infant later.[1]

An Atmosphere of Warmth
In the months before birth the first foundation stone for the child's life is laid—the cornerstone of trust. It's vitally important to secure this trust after the birth and to continue cultivating it. Again, the relationship between Father and Mother has the effect of either affirming the incipient trust or shattering it.

When the young child hears Father and Mother confess to each other, "I love you," he or she is wrapped in a profound sense of security and safety. This simple statement can have an almost magical effect.

But the parents' love has to be seen in action as well. It isn't enough for Father to say the words and then leave the difficult work of child care to Mother while he takes it easy on the sofa.

When a mother knows that her husband loves her, she is more likely to be open and affectionate with her children. But if she feels rejected, she's apt to be curt and undemonstrative in her mothering. It often happens that the pent-up feelings that should be directed toward the husband are instead vented on the children.

Clearly, then, a father has an indirect influence on his children through his relationship with their mother. And a mother can enhance this influence. Her words can be like a mirror in which the children see their father.

The Father in the Mirror

A young child accepts every word a grown-up says as indisputable fact. In fact, doubt is foreign to a child's nature. Later, when he or she has learned through negative experience not to believe everything people say, the child will become less trusting and more cautious.

In the first months it is the mother who speaks most to the child. The child is initiated into the world through her, even though he doesn't always understand the meaning of her words. A caring mother will talk about things that delight the child. She will look at the clouds with him, and at animals. She will comment on the cars and people that go by, and talk about all sorts of other things.

But she'll also spend much time talking about the person who binds them together: the father. Perhaps he has just gone out the door on his way to work. Then the mother takes the child in her arms and they wave bye-bye through the window. The child watches his daddy get into the car and drive away.

To make the separation easier, the mother now tells the child what Daddy does at work and how eager he will be to return home after work to play with his child. Again and again the mother will speak his name very clearly: Pa-pa or Dad-dy. And the child tries to imitate the sounds he hears.

It's a most wonderful moment for Daddy when he comes home one day and hears his child trying to say his name. A stranger will not appreciate this effort. Only the father himself can. Children whose first word is "Papa" or "Daddy" show that a close relationship exists between the father and the mother—because here is proof that Mommy has talked about her husband a great deal.

When our children were still small and Michiaki had to be off at a conference for several days, the waiting period was filled with the anticipation of his homecoming. Each day was focused on him. Again and again the children described in great detail what they could do to welcome him home. An old sheet became a flag that showed not only the red sun of Japan but also many colorful figures dancing happily. And all day long the children heard about their father, until evening, when they were allowed to sleep in Daddy's bed, convinced that they had the best father in the whole wide world.

The faces that greeted him upon his return were all aglow. As he entered the house the children leaped upon him in delight, their flag fluttering forgotten to the floor. And then they had to give account of every single event he had missed, and he unpacked the little surprises he had brought to show he had been thinking of them, too, while he was away.

These happy interactions are the result when Father is mirrored in the words that Mother speaks. There is a similar effect when a child hears his father praised by a neighbor or a teacher. Little ones feel deeply pleased when their father is respected by others, when his work or his character is honored.

The Power of Negative Words

Just as positive talk has a positive influence, negative talk has a profound effect on the child. So a mother must weigh her words very carefully before she speaks.

It may be that her husband has disappointed her. Perhaps she has separated from him. But in spite of everything, he is still the children's father.

A mother may not feel strong enough to be in charge of her children. So she casts about for help, something she can use to give her words more weight. Most mothers nowadays are unlikely to use the "bogeyman" as a threat to gain their children's compliance. But the bogeyman may still be alive and well under a different name. For some it's God: "God will punish you if you don't . . ." Or "If you do that, Jesus will be very sad." How does she know? Can she honestly say that God is hurt by childish defiance? And if she doesn't know, why does she say it?

This mother would be more in accord with reality if she said, "I am upset with you because you have done this or that." After all, her child must learn to judge his behavior correctly. Now he knows: Mother is angry when I behave like this.

Here is another damaging appeal to the bogeyman: "Just you wait till your father comes home!" This mother's child knows full well what is in store. And it's not surprising that he doesn't look forward to his father's return home.

When a mother hides behind her husband and uses his authority to get the children to mind her, she shouldn't be surprised when the children start seeing him as an enemy. The child's imagination then enlarges this enemy-image, making it gigantic, until his perception of reality is affected by it. So for a mother to use such a battle tactic is unfair; the damage her strategy causes has no bounds.

Actually, it makes no sense for the child to wait until Dad comes home from work; Mom can take care of the matter quite spontaneously and on the spot. A firm smack can be a palpable sign that a boundary was crossed and that there are consequences. Then the matter is closed. And when Dad comes home from work, the child can run to greet him with a light heart.

A mother's negative speech about her husband is deeply destructive for her children. But when she blesses her husband with positive talk, she helps open the way for the children to have a warm, trusting relationship with their father.

8

THE FATHER AS ROLE MODEL

Gateway to the World

It was wonderful to watch. The little boy next door was helping his big, burly father push a heavy wheelbarrow. And when Dad began digging in the garden, the son had a shovel, too. Later, when the attic needed to be finished, the boy was right there, hammer in hand, face shining with pride. Just like his dad. No matter where the father went, his little son followed him like a shadow.

You could see that the boy was proud of his father. When he rode into the house on his father's shoulders, his triumphant smile seemed to say, "My dad can do anything!"

Learning Through Imitation

For a small child, Father is a model to imitate. The child wants to slip into his father's skin, as it were. Haven't we all seen a comical picture of a little guy plodding around in his father's shoes, with the long sleeves of his father's jacket hanging almost to the floor—and the boy's beaming smile, so proud to wear Dad's things?

Children observe. They want to imitate, and so to learn. They want to be like the one they look up to.

The urge to imitate is innate in a child, no matter how distinctive his or her personality. Through imitation children learn to become themselves and to find their own way. This is why children need someone they can admire. They need a hero, a strong guy who can't be outsmarted.

They are going to learn the most from whomever they love. Therefore, each child needs a father.

When Father drags himself grumbling out of bed, sullenly gulps down his coffee and heads off cursing to a job he hates, what image is he conveying to his child? The child can't possibly develop any positive attitude toward work from an example like this. On the other hand, when a father enjoys his work, is careful to be punctual and makes good on his word, his children will quite naturally assume these traits.

Modeling Relationships

If a father believes that once he is home he can just let himself go, excusing himself with the reminder that he has had to be on his good behavior all day at work, he is sadly mistaken. If he loses control of himself at work, it's not as bad as losing his cool at home. At work he is interacting with adults—near strangers. But at home he is followed by the eyes of his own child, who consciously or unconsciously registers everything he does and takes that as an example to follow.

If children notice that their dad isn't particularly careful about telling the truth, soon they too will start to lie. And it won't be long before distorting or withholding the truth is habitual for them. Parents are generally horrified by their children's lies. But didn't they plant the seed of this behavior by using lies to get themselves off the hook?

Conversely, when a father acts out his belief that telling the truth is important, children will take delight in telling the truth themselves.

Children also notice how Daddy talks to Mommy. When a father acts lovingly and considerately, speaking to his wife in a quiet, respectful tone, the children will follow his lead. But if he puts his wife down in front of the children, they will soon lose all respect for her and will yell at her just as Daddy does.

When children hear their father thank Mother for a delicious meal, they will learn to say thank you to her too. And later, when they themselves are married, these habits of daily politeness will continue. Small gestures—how they color our daily lives! *Thank you* is such a short, simple phrase, but it goes far to create an atmosphere of warmth and generosity.

A father can hardly expect self-control from his children if he cannot control himself. He must set the example. In the same way, renunciation will remain an abstract virtue for children unless Dad shows that he can forgo his own wishes without becoming resentful.

Children will learn to forgive if they are exposed to a model who practices the art of forgiveness. If Dad is willing to give up his own advantage for the sake of a greater good, his children will stop striving for self-gratification and evaluating all things according to their own preferences.

What a father is, what he does, how he acts and talks—all of this will be picked up by his children.

Looking for a Hero

What good is the most expensive education, with up-to-date knowledge of psychology, if a man himself falls short? As a person, a man, a friend, a *father,* Dad is the living example his children watch and after whom they pattern themselves. He is like an anchor that holds his children. As the children survey the outside world, taking stock of it before they try their wings, it's Father who gives them the security and confidence they need.

The trend today is to ignore all boundaries. You'd better do everything right, or you'll get sued. Insurance companies work out huge cash settlements. Epithets are hurled back and forth. People seem addicted to criticizing.

This is the kind of world children see when they look beyond their families. But what they want to find is someone they can identify with—a hero. They try out heroes—talking like them, dressing like them, acting like them. Heroes figure in their daydreams. Television heroes, pop stars, whoever is "in" can become a hero. But when children see that their father is a person who acts differently, thinks differently and lives differently, they will have the courage to be themselves and take delight in their individuality.

Defining the Limits

In school, children learn quite early that they have power. And they will be taught to use this power—sometimes even against their parents. But actually children are not ready for this. They don't want power; instead, they are looking for security. And security is possible only in submission. Strict boundaries must be erected to give children security, and within these defined limits their selves can begin to unfold.

This is why children need their father.

Today children are bombarded nonstop with more televised pictures and noise than they can process. Some are pictures they don't know what to do with. War, violence, sex, perversion—everything takes place before children's eyes. Fascinated by the motion, they can't tear themselves away. Pictures and events fly past in a frantic jumble, leaving the little ones wounded deep in their souls.

Children are vulnerable to sounds and images; they have no way to protect themselves. It's very hard for children to find their way through today's maze of advertisements. The child is an identified consumer and is thus very significant for the economy. Producers of children's goods vie for their preferences and their spending money. And many children today have small fortunes at their disposal. Again, they need Father to teach them how to cope with all the temptations. A father's example shapes his child's way of "doing business."

Building Primal Trust

To show how a father serves as his children's "gateway to the world," we need to review stages of development in a young child. The well-known psychoanalyst Erik Erikson labels the first months of an infant's life, when she is totally dependent on the mother, the *symbiotic phase*. During this time, "primal trust" is developed.[1] This primal trust is rooted deep in the child's personhood and determines, to a great extent, the direction her life will take. If the child experiences security in this decisive phase, she will trust others more easily later on. If, instead, she experiences disappointment, the primal trust is shaky.

The foundation for this primal trust is laid in the mother's womb, and after birth it is fostered primarily by the mother. She is the one who creates the first relationship with the child, who nourishes and cares for the little one. Her constant nearness and attentiveness give the child a sense of security. The baby is safe, relaxed, satisfied.

Mother's responses to the child, as we have noted, are likely to be greatly affected by her environment. If, for example, her marriage is plagued by persistent problems, she cannot give the child her full attention. She will be nervous and distracted, and these feelings will be communicated to her child. The child in turn feels insecure and becomes fussy—the first awakening of mistrust.

In these first months a child needs consistency and attention, in particular from her mother. She needs to be talked to, to have Mommy's physical presence. When the child makes her own presence known—and crying is her only way to do so—Mommy is there. She talks to the child, smiles at her, calms her, takes her in her arms. The little one senses the warmth and safety that Mommy provides. And, naturally, she would like to enjoy this presence as long as possible.

Sometimes an infant is left to cry for hours, and may even be put in another room with the door closed so that her "rebellious spirit" will be broken. But there is great danger that this will break her sense of trust as well. Crying is the only language an infant has. So Mommy should answer her cries—but at the same time the little one should be trained so that she doesn't develop into a tyrant. Fortunately, most mothers quickly learn to discern what the baby wants to express through crying.

Stepping into Safety

From the fifth through the ninth month the infant is in the *differentiation phase,* according to psychoanalysts Margaret S. Mahler and Ernest L. Abelin.[2] This is the first phase of separation. The baby begins to discover her own world; she perceives other people and objects. She tries to grasp everything and put it into her mouth—to taste the world!

The period from the ninth to the fourteenth month can be called the child's *practicing phase.* During this time the child learns a new basis for security: Daddy. Father and mother are one unit, because they love each other; yet Daddy is a different person, not identical with Mommy. He is close by, but his nearness is experienced differently.

The child stretches out her little arms toward Daddy—and thereby lets go of Mommy. The father takes the child into his arms, and she quickly twists around and leans with outstretched arms toward Mommy—or perhaps she chooses to stay with Daddy. It's like a game, moving from one to the other.

Daddy is there as a second person who is close to the child and provides security. In his arms she is surrounded by strength—a different kind of security.

When the child sees that Daddy and Mommy get along well and are in harmony with each other, it's very easy for her to exchange one for the other. She feels secure with her mother, but she also feels safe with her father. So Mommy can go shopping without her child getting upset. Daddy is there, all is well.

When the father is not there, however, the child has no one except her mother. She belongs totally to Mommy. And at some point the child would like to free herself from being her mother's possession. She wants Mommy close, yet turns away from her.

Opening Up the World

From the fifteenth to the twenty-fourth month most children have a renewed attachment to their mother. In this "back-to-mother" phase, the child is quite ambivalent. The parents see the child being pulled in two directions, and they interpret it as defiance or displeasure. Actually, the "defiance" is part of normal development and is age-related. The child wants to and doesn't want to. She seeks security but at the same time wants to be free. She resists connection to her mother, yet a moment later she returns to this oneness.

Again it's the father who comes to help the child in this difficult time of indecision. He takes her on a kind of discovery tour, opening up new worlds to the little one. He talks to her, shows her interesting things to play with, tries out new games with her. The child is fascinated. She crows with enthusiasm.

Around the eighteenth month the child discovers herself. She learns to distinguish herself from Daddy and Mommy; her self-consciousness awakens. As the child's ego develops, her parents hear her saying, "Me do it!" or "I want to!"

If Mommy tries to hold the child back, to guide her into the old familiar patterns, Daddy is there to encourage the child to strike out on her own. This basic pattern repeats itself countless times—and from day to day the child's confidence in her own abilities increases. Thus a father guides his child gradually toward independence.

When the father isn't there, the child has a hard time developing a sense of self. She's likely to remain dependent on Mother for a long time. We frequently encounter grown sons and daughters who are still being babied by their mothers. They think the mother's thoughts and feel her feelings. They have never managed to "cut the cord." The result is a crippled life, unhappy, static, weighed down with depression and fear until everything seems quite meaningless. Having spent their lives imprisoned, these sons and daughters have had no chance to put their own capabilities to the test.

It is the father's responsibility not only to loosen this symbiotic tie with the mother but also to open up new worlds to the child, worlds that the child can conquer. Father will show the child how to cope in the big, wide world without getting hurt. For he trains the child and prepares her for the difficulties that lie ahead.

9

THE FATHER AS DISCIPLINARIAN
Building Self-Control

*I*n *the process of becoming an individual, a child strives for autonomy.* Seeking to discover himself, he tests the limits to see how far he can stretch them. When he encounters an obstacle that limits his range of motion, he tries to conquer the obstacle, to expand his space. He wants to be master not only of himself but also of his surroundings. He wants to be in control of everything and controlled by nothing and no one. In fact, he wishes to be absolute ruler.

Breaking or Guiding?
After the initial formation of self-awareness, which is completed by about eighteen months of age, the child is entirely focused on himself. Everything he tries out is related to his egocentric needs. He wants this thing but also covets that thing. He screams when he doesn't get

his way. The first conflicts with the world around him surface at this stage. The child tries hard to get others to give in. He wants to emerge the winner in every power struggle, and he becomes frustrated and aggressive when his efforts don't pay off.

His parents are worn out. The strain of the day has taken a toll, and they'd like to have some time for themselves. But here is the little troublemaker, who has no qualms whatsoever about raising a ruckus. He wants to be the center of attention. Mommy and Daddy are supposed to be there for him and focus only on his wants and needs.

Soon parents and child may come into conflict about a new aspect of development: toilet training. Opinions on this matter vary widely from culture to culture. Basically, however, all parents must realize that a child's sphincter muscles cannot be regulated before age eighteen months to two years, so no toilet training should be attempted before the child is at least a year and a half old.

This *anal phase* is fundamental for the formation of a child's will. Cooperation between parents and child is crucial at this time so that the child does not suffer shame. It would be counterproductive and, in fact, wrong to try to "break" the child's will by force. The point is to guide him onto the right path. You see, the child will need his will later on; his will is a source of strength. Breaking it would mean bringing on a kind of early paralysis that would leave him vulnerable to harm later.

The older the child becomes, the more visible and audible he is. Soon he doesn't lie in his bed like a "good little boy" but instead runs all over the house, getting into everything and resisting correction. Mother is on guard constantly, ready to pull him away from any imminent danger or to rescue a fragile object from his possessive grasp. The child can't see the danger and can't understand why Mommy grabs the knife from his hand or lifts him down from the table where he was about to investigate the big bowl steaming with an enticing aroma. He only wanted to see where the intriguing wisps of steam came from. It isn't fair; he protests loudly.

The Father's Discipline

If the child hasn't learned to back off after two warnings, and then a third, Mom disciplines him with a smack on the bottom. He is first puzzled, then shocked and indignant. In spite of this unpleasant experience, however, the compulsion is still there. And then it happens: the precious vase is lying in pieces, or the bowl is overturned on the floor and its contents are soaking into the carpet.

Mom scolds. She is angry. She may even be beside herself, overwhelmed. All her warnings were in vain. Unfortunately, now she may cast about for a more effective technique to put the fear of God into the child: "Just you wait till your father gets home!"

And when Daddy comes home, the child hides, for he is afraid.

As we've explained, a mother should not resort to threats of later punishment from Father. But she may be tempted to do so because this strategy seems to work over the short term. There is a reason for that.

Discipline meted out by fathers apparently has a longer-lasting effect than mothers' discipline. According to H. B. Biller, males are regarded as having greater ability to establish limits.[1] It has often been observed that boys are disciplined by their fathers more often than girls are. This can be healthy for a boy, fostering his sense of masculinity—provided that his father has made the limits unmistakably clear and communicates caring along with the discipline.

If Father does not discipline in love, the punishment will have an effect that is opposite from what was intended: it will engender aggressive behavior. And if the punishment is motivated by a certain sense of superiority and is carried out with an air of triumph, the child will suffer deep emotional harm. Aware of his powerlessness, he is forced to hide his massive fury. His rage may actually be repressed for years—but all the while it is growing in intensity, until one day it forces its way to the surface and explodes. Then a delayed revenge may be executed on the person who caused his anger in the first place, or perhaps on society at large, which seems to represent the father.

When the law is laid down too forcefully, children feel like captives. When a father loses his temper and yells at his child or strikes out in blind fury, this will not be perceived as discipline but as subjugation. The child is no match for his parents' superior power, so he adapts. Yet he chafes under the harsh treatment, and his self-esteem suffers. Unjust punishments or explosions of uncontrolled rage can pierce a child's soul like a thorn and fester there. A certain bitterness of heart grows within him. In later stages of his development the excessively punished child becomes either unsure of himself or cruel.

Any correction must be carried out in love. The discipline must always fit the child and must never get out of hand. Also, it should be administered immediately after a misdeed is discovered—not later. And the child should be told exactly why he is being disciplined. In general, a child will accept a just discipline without resisting.

If it turns out that a punishment was unfair, it goes without saying that the father or mother—whoever was responsible—should apologize to the child. In such an instance the punishment can be seen as a kind of IOU for the next offense. As a rule, children will gladly cooperate in working out a deal, as long as they recognize sincerity and love in their parents.

The Importance of Discipline

There is no one prescription that works for everyone, but we say with certainty that loving discipline not only helps the parents but also is helpful for the child. When there are no consequences for inappropriate behavior, children learn no self-control. The child of anti-authoritarian parents has an exaggerated sense of his own importance and will seize any opportunity to bully others.

According to the Swiss psychologist Jean Piaget, a child's moral standards are "under construction" until he reaches the age of eleven or twelve.[2] If a father's discipline has been absent up to this age, it will be very difficult later to correct the standards that the child has adopted from outside the home.

Disciplining a child does not mean destroying his confidence; on the contrary, the child senses that he is being taken seriously. Sometimes a child may even wait to be punished. When he receives his punishment, he has the feeling that he has been treated justly. So we see that appropriate discipline can help form a child's sense of fairness.

But what does it mean that "discipline must be carried out in love"? In the moment of anger, love is not exactly foremost in a father's consciousness, yet love is what compels him to discipline in the first place. The decisive factor, then, is Father's basic attitude toward his child. If the father has accepted his child lovingly, then his anger will not diminish this love. For his love doesn't depend on his child's behavior. The child remains his child, regardless of the behavior.

A loving father is his child's ally. And *because* he loves this child, he will simply not accept certain kinds of behavior. Instead, he will use fatherly reprimands to help the youngster overcome his weaknesses.

Shaping a Young Life
A builder must have a plan before starting to build. And likewise, fathers would do well to ask themselves, "What kind of person do I want my child to grow up to be?" Of course Dad won't sit down and, like an architect, make a sketch of all the character traits he would like to instill in his children. But he will—perhaps unconsciously—

carry a mental picture and try to conform his children to it. As a rule, he will pass on to his children his own concept of life and his own goals. He knows how difficult it is for many young people to find their way as they become adults. So he would like to see his children become integrated into society and be accepted rather than rejected. He'd like to help form persons who relate well to others and have a place in the community.

How should he pursue this goal?

First of all, he needs to strengthen and cultivate his children's confidence. We have already spoken of the foundation upon which a child's life should be built. Part of this foundation is the parents' harmonious marriage, and another part is the father's love and caring. These elements create an atmosphere that allows a child to be relaxed. Free from undue fear, he can experience delight in all the little things that surround him. This delight is another important building block in the child's life. After this comes the necessity of directing the will and guiding it in the right path.

When a child is quite young, the criteria of *right* and *wrong* are not part of his consciousness.[3] He doesn't know what is good and what isn't. Although we have observed that many children seem to act instinctively according to an inner sense of what is good and what is bad, it's still clear that a child learns through his interaction with other people. In order to escape a punishment perceived as unpleasant, the child avoids whatever Dad and Mom call "bad." Parents, then, have an important role in shaping the young conscience.

At first a deed will be perceived as good if it satisfies the child's need. Whatever is pleasant appears to be good. But this childish criterion doesn't necessarily agree with his parents' standards—and conflicts occur. Again the child has to learn. Since it's pleasant to be praised, he seeks this reward.

Eventually, however, he doesn't behave merely according to the principle of praise or punishment but uses his own reasoning ability to develop new criteria for evaluating his behavior. In this phase, disagreements with his father are significant. It must be made clear to him: when you act in this way, this will be the result. The father represents society. This process teaches a child to obey laws, fulfill obligations and make a positive contribution to the human community.

The Golden Rule, "Do to others what you would have them do to you," must be instilled in a child while he is very young. This saves the child—and society—from many unpleasant conflicts and crises.

Going Against the Grain

Wherever the Golden Rule is ignored and the pleasure principle is followed instead, a person oversteps his bounds. He becomes *guilty.*

Many people today insist that guilt should be done away with and pleasure should be acknowledged as a right. When this view is carried to its logical conclusions, abortion is legalized and promiscuity becomes the norm. Individuals want to be the final authority, to determine for themselves what is good and what is evil. Yet determining good and evil does not lie within the province of the human will. This is why the father's parenting role is vital.

If a father is a Christian, his moral code and ethical standards will be influenced by the Bible. And the Bible's moral code is totally contrary to today's philosophy of life.

When Jesus speaks of love in the Sermon on the Mount (Mt 5:43-48), he is talking about a total commitment of oneself to God. Only through this total commitment will a person become capable of loving.

Human beings want to get rid of suffering—to shut out everything that causes discomfort. But Jesus said those who bear suffering are happy.

Human beings want to conquer the world by force. But Jesus promised the meek that they would possess the earth.

Mercy is a quality that is often ridiculed and interpreted as weakness. But in the Bible, mercy is an important quality of God's character.

Because God cannot be perceived through human eyes, he has been declared dead. But Jesus said, "Whoever is pure in heart shall see God."

Everyone talks about peace, but they want it on their own terms and will bring it about by force, if need be. But Jesus blessed the peacemakers, those who use peaceful means to bring harmony and reconciliation.

Justice is in every mouth; yet people do violence to what is right. But Jesus calls us to hunger and thirst for God's justice.

There are calls on every side for retribution. But Jesus invites us to learn forgiveness.

Given the world's resistance to every biblical standard, it's not easy to take Jesus' way. That's why children need their fathers' moral guidance.

Some examples from the Bible clearly show the importance of paternal discipline. In 1 Kings 1:6 we read why Adonijah, David's son, rebelled in anger at his father: "His father had never interfered with him by asking, 'Why do you behave as you do?' " Fatherly correction was utterly lacking. And the lack cost Adonijah his life (1 Kings 2:13-25).

A similar fate befell the family of Eli the priest. In this case the father brought the judgment of God upon his house because "of the sin he knew about; his sons made themselves contemptible, and he failed to restrain them" (1 Sam 3:13). Eli failed as a parent. In an attempt to protect his sons, he remained silent and so brought misfortune upon his whole family.

Children need to be brought up in a way that promotes self-control and, along with it, self-respect. In this way a father strengthens his children's ability to resist temptation.

Flexible and Practical Rules

In a family, as in society, there are certain rules that must be obeyed. These rules are first of all a means of protection and must be taught to children as age permits. Particularly in the "I want" phase, parents must decide what they will allow and what they will not. Some rules must be obeyed strictly, while with others a degree of flexibility is possible.

Child rearing should always be practical. A child first learns to abide by the rules of play. He learns to distinguish between "mine" and "yours." He learns to verbalize a wish as a question or a request: "May I please have this or that?"

As parents teach these practical rules of behavior, it's important that they focus on each child individually. Yet they must make sure that they don't give another child grounds to feel neglected or unfairly treated.

One child is not like the next. Parents want to be fair, yet they must take the individual character of each child into consideration. They will treat a timid child differently from a bold one. One small word of criticism will cause great anguish for an overly conscientious child, whereas his brother will get over a vehement scolding in five minutes.

The discipline of children needs to be thought through and balanced out so as to avoid too much strictness and too much indulgence. A father must be neither too cool nor too warm. Closeness and distance are both necessary. Too much closeness stifles, but too little warmth causes a child to close up and grow inward. A child's space must be large enough for him to test his own strengths, and small enough for him to know the boundaries.

10

THE FATHER AS A MAN

Sacrificial Strength

*W*e have seen that children see father and mother as a unit and at the same time distinguish one from the other. So what is the essence of the difference between father and mother? Is it only a biological distinction, or is there some important difference in character? Is it just that Daddy has a deep voice and rough skin?

What do we mean by the term *manliness*? Is a real man "Mr. Muscle," like TV's pro wrestlers, or a gallant type no woman can resist? Is he the wealthy businessman who spares no expense when entertaining his friends? What does it mean that a father is a *man*?

The lines of definition of the sexes have been obscured in our time by the interchanging of roles. The mechanization of industry has largely equalized what used to be gender-specific. The home used to be a woman's realm; today, however, schools encourage boys to take courses in cooking and other domestic arts, while girls may learn auto mechanics if they wish. There is no difference now between the barber shop and the beauty salon; it is all unisex. Nowadays it isn't just the mother who gets maternity leave from work; the father also applies for paternity leave to spend time with his newborn. Many married men are staying home long-term, too, as house-husbands. How, then, can a boy or girl find a role with which to identify?

Courage and Confidence

In using the term *manly,* people usually are referring to the traditional male role of protector, the one who puts his life on the line for wife and family, the selfless father who sacrifices himself for his children, the courageous one who does not shrink from any danger and who stands firm in his convictions, even when all others oppose him and he stands alone.

In 1 Kings 2:2, King David commanded his son, "Be strong, show yourself a man." A mother may use the word *man* in the same way when she exhorts her son to "be a man"—meaning "Bear the pain without complaining!"

In Job 38:3 God challenges Job, "Brace yourself like a man." Here the word *man* is associated with courage, fearlessness and self-confidence.

Self-confidence is not to be equated with self-righteousness and obstinacy. Self-confidence holds within it a calm certainty that all will be well, a positive sense of expectancy, the conviction that all problems can be dealt with. This is not arrogance, but an assurance that a workable solution can be found.

A father who communicates self-confidence knows his own value. He doesn't need to brag about it and doesn't need to lord it over others. But he doesn't allow himself to be intimidated or compromised in any way.

Gentleness and Self-Control

Yet no man is called to be a superman. Countless examples in Scripture bear this out. Peter weeps out of bitter disappointment in himself, but that does not diminish his manliness; instead, it allows him to reveal his humanness. And Paul is not ashamed to speak of the times he despaired of life (2 Cor 1:8).

A man is permitted to tremble and be filled with despair. A man may weep without compromising his manliness. A man may be wrong and make mistakes. But he may not stop there and give up.

A man is capable of keeping silent. An old proverb says, "A man of understanding holds his tongue" (Prov 11:12). He does not flaunt his intelligence in order to gain attention (Prov 12:23).

A healthy man is distinguished by patience. This means he can wait, even when the result isn't apparent right away. And a patient man will not be quarrelsome; instead, he will seek reconciliation (Prov 15:18). Where anger fuels the flames of argument, the wise man will step in as mediator (Prov 16:14). Yet when it is necessary, this same wise man will show his anger and will even take drastic steps to right what is wrong (Jn 2:13-16).

Manliness is not represented only by fearlessness and strength; a mature man is capable of great tenderness and sensitivity toward his wife. With her he is loving, generous, understanding and kind. The patriarch Jacob, for example, is characterized in the Old Testament as a "quiet" (or "gentle") man (Gen 25:27). Jesus says of himself, "I am gentle and humble in heart" (Mt 11:29). Thus, some traits that usually are attributed to women are actually quite masculine, according to Scripture.

Finally, a key characteristic of manliness is self-discipline. What makes a man a man, in the last analysis, is the ability to bring his passions under control. Giving free rein to one's temperament is a sign not of masculinity but of weakness. A man must have learned to master himself, to tame his passions. To tolerate stress and tension. To put others first.

When a father is a man in this sense of the word, he will also be manly in his profession—that is, he will shoulder his responsibility and not only stand up for his own rights but make his contribution to the community as well. He will not be an impractical dreamer but will judge situations realistically.

A truly masculine man complements his wife. This complementarity is necessary, because it represents balance within the family.

The Complementarity of the Sexes

Although all godly fathers and mothers are called to cultivate every positive character quality, these qualities are expressed differently, or have different emphases, in men and women.

Taking a look at the characteristics that are considered typically feminine, we would begin with *motherliness*. This quality encompasses warmth, the ability to convey security, a certain softness, something comforting and comfortable. These traits are also found in men, and they serve to underscore a man's masculinity. But they are not *primary* traits of a man. A father does convey a sense of security, but it is mainly communicated to his child through manly strength.

A mother is often "soft" and yielding. This doesn't mean that she changes her no to a yes at the least sign of resistance. But it does mean that she doesn't get hung up on principles; she is flexible, able to "tune in" to her child. A good father needs to have this ability also, but as a man he will demonstrate firmness without being rigid, decisiveness without being stubborn.

A father's love looks a bit different from a mother's love. A mother tolerates, endures, suffers long for the sake of her child, does not become discouraged; she loves without expecting anything for herself. Whereas the mother's love is characterized by tenderness and warmheartedness, the father's love is expressed primarily through guidance.

The woman is the adaptable one, the receiver, the conceiver and bearer; in security she can offer security. The man is like a retaining wall, surrounding his family and preventing its dissolution. As the head, he lays down rules. Therefore his praise means more to the children and his reproach weighs heavier; his affirmation encourages the children and gives his wife renewed strength.

When the Bible speaks of man's "headship" (for example, Eph 5:21-33), it is never referring to domination. Men are not born to rule by virtue of having the loudest voice. For woman is not less than man; she is not his subordinate, not a maidservant created to wait on him hand and foot. Rather, God has entrusted her to him to watch over and to love—just as Christ loves his church. Then she can be to him the helper she was meant to be from the beginning of creation.

It's in *this* sense that a man is head of his family. If a man loves his wife and accepts her as she is, then the atmosphere in their family will be wholesome and happy. In turn, a woman needs to encourage her husband's manliness so that the qualities within him may become visible.

Whoever wishes to be a good father to his children must first of all learn to be a good man. If he fails in this, he will also fail in relation to his children.

Modeling Manliness

As early as 1953, P. S. Sears made the observation that a warm father-son relationship in early childhood fosters a boy's masculinity.[1] And the overwhelming majority of later studies confirm this finding. This means that fatherly affection coupled with consistent discipline helps sons grow up to be manly men with good social skills.

Generally, a father does not treat all his children the same. It seems as though in most cultures fathers prefer sons over daughters. First-born sons have a special place in many cultures. They have a distinctive position as heirs and enjoy their fathers' special favor. They are their fathers' pride and joy. But the more sons a father can produce, the greater his feeling of self-worth. He lives on, as it were, in his sons. In some cultures it is sons who perpetuate the veneration of ancestors after their father's death.

Many fathers greet the birth of a son with great and obvious enthusiasm, whereas they react to the birth of a daughter more quietly. And fathers seem more willing to help care for their infant if it is a boy. This continues to be the case as the child grows older. The father's unconscious focusing on his son leads the boy, quite naturally, to become particularly attached to his father.

A father's masculinity is expressed through the way he handles his children. It's usually Mother who feeds and cares for the children; a father is more likely to interact with his children through play. And games with Daddy are different from playing with Mommy. Her play tends to be gentle and quiet; she sings, tells stories, reads aloud. Daddy, on the other hand, enjoys roughhousing; he throws his son up in the air, spins him around, sees who can crawl the fastest or challenges the little guy to a wrestling match.

For playthings, fathers are most likely to choose mechanical toys, whereas mothers might pick dolls. So a mother introduces her daughter to the feminine world, and a father prepares his son for the masculine world. It's not surprising, then, that from age two on sons show a definite preference for games with Daddy. By contrast, daughters turn from their father somewhere between ages two and four and choose to play with Mom.

We can see that play is of great significance in sexual identification. Mother communicates feminine behaviors, and Father models what is masculine. When a father tumbles with his little son and rigs up

Tinker Toy contraptions, the son will imitate him. Daddy is his model, his example, his hero. The little son wants to be just like Daddy when he grows up.

Fathers and Daughters

But fathers are important for daughters' development as well. If a father notices clearly masculine traits in his daughter, he will instinctively try to correct them and will praise her when he sees her taking after her mother. In this way he helps his daughter become more feminine and affirms her femininity through his praise. Fathers help differentiate between masculine and feminine behaviors and clarify healthy gender roles for their children.

Father is the first man in a little girl's life. She makes an effort to please him. Her efforts, in fact, can lead to a silent rivalry between mother and daughter—the so-called Electra complex. But when a daughter identifies closely with her mother, who in turn is loved deeply by her husband, the girl grows more easily into her feminine identity.

A good relationship between father and daughter can be extremely important later, when she is ready to make decisions about marriage. The converse is also true: a problematic relationship between father and daughter can place a great burden on her, so that she has a hard time finding a good marriage partner. For example, we've observed that daughters of alcoholics tend to marry alcoholics. The father-daughter relationship naturally develops into a set of unconscious criteria for making choices in dealing with men. So fathers play a critical role not only in their sons' gender consciousness but also in their daughters' search for identity.

Teaching About Sex

It is the father's responsibility to enlighten his son about sexual matters, man to man. And it is the mother's place to explain matters of sexuality to her daughter.

The first conversation about questions of sex should take place when the child is very young, and there should be no erotic allusions. Questions should be answered as candidly as they are asked. Usually a young child is satisfied with just a few simple explanations.

Later, when a child enters adolescence and is confronted with his or her own sexuality, another conversation will take place. This time it will go into more detail. Sharing like this draws parent and child close in a special way. But again, it's important that the conversation be confined to facts and that moralizing be kept out of it.

We consider it very important that information about sex be given initially by parents rather than by schools. Sex education in a mixed group in a classroom has inherent problems. The teacher must have a special kind of empathy to meet this challenge. Often in these settings, children are given far more information than they're able to comprehend. It's fine for children to be amazed and astonished, but their imaginations should not be burdened needlessly.

The more young people learn about the use of contraceptives, for example, the more they will feel almost expected to try them out. And allusions to sexual pleasure have no appropriate place in the classroom.

It's our opinion that mandatory sex education in schools has done more harm than good, and that it will take until well into the next generation for the negative effect to work itself out. So parents should be alert and should speak with their children's teachers before sex-education sessions come up. They should insist on being informed in advance of the form and content of any discussions of physical sexuality.

But teaching about sex is just one part of a father's teaching responsibility. In the next chapter we'll widen our focus to see how fathers are suited—and called—to teach their children about life.

11

THE FATHER AS TEACHER

A Firm but Gentle Guide

*I*n *general,* instruction *is a major part of child rearing. If parents focus* mainly on behavior as they train their children, placing a great emphasis on moral values, then the father's and mother's own intellect and values will surely be challenged and tested. In this way child rearing is a crucible of truth.

All parents find that their children begin questioning at a very early age. Everything must be explained: Why is the sun round? Why doesn't the moon fall from the sky? Why do birds have wings? Why does a hen peck food with her beak? Why does Grandma have white hair, while Mother's is brown? Why, why, why?

The father's teaching task can be examined from three perspectives: (1) When does he instruct? (2) What does he teach? (3) How does he teach?

When Does a Father Teach?

Each father must grow into his task. Instinct and experience tell him when he should talk with his child. There is no set moment that instruction begins.

An infant starts developing awareness of surroundings from the beginning, and these impressions are stored up. At six months the child begins to babble. She tries to imitate noises. Then come the first word-symbols that have real meaning. How proud Daddy and Mommy are when they understand their child's first word! Perhaps no outsider could make sense of it, but the parents have grasped what the child is trying to say. In the first two years, children learn about two hundred words. It is said that their linguistic ability reaches its peak around the age of five. Between the ages of three and six, language and imagination develop, and most children are ready for school by age six. According to the stages identified by Erik Erikson, a child is most open to intellectual development between the ages of six and thirteen. This is a challenging time for parents.

Since Mother is likely the one who spends the greater part of the day with the little children, she has the greatest influence on their early acquisition of language. But the children also need to interact with Daddy.

Perhaps a father assumes that his child understands so little that it isn't necessary to spend a lot of time with her. As long as she is kept clean and is fed regularly, she ought to be content. But children are not cars—machines that just need regular maintenance. They possess the ability to learn, they can be influenced by others, and they react to the ways they are approached and treated. A child is happy when Mommy and Daddy talk with her, sing to her, read to her and have patience with her. When she recognizes that Mommy and Daddy understand her, she is happy.

It takes time to listen. Waving a child away impatiently or displaying an unwillingness to pay attention to her creates anxiety. And anxiety causes a child to close up.

So when Father notices that his child is interested in something, he should seize the opportunity to listen to her concerns and to teach her.

What Does a Father Teach?

First of all, a father needs to teach his child manual skills. This begins very early, when Daddy shows the child how to put one block on top of another, so that a tall tower soon takes shape before the child's delighted eyes. When the child bumps against it, the tower comes crashing down, and now the game can start over from the beginning. Next, little cars are assembled from Lego pieces; perhaps an airplane comes next, depending on the father's interests.

The child needs to learn to handle different materials. To foster learning ability, it's better to choose simple toys that can be manipulated than those that need only to be steered. This will encourage a child to busy herself creatively. Toys that are finished products are not especially interesting; there isn't much she can do with or to them. Imagination needs possibilities if it is to develop. It may be better to give a little boy plain chunks of wood or plastic so that he can create his own world, rather than a remote-controlled car that needs only the press of a button for operation. Sometimes a cardboard box, crayons and scissors will suffice for the creation of a magical world of pretend.

If a child has shelves full of toys and gets one of every new kind that is advertised on television, she'll get in the habit of wanting new toys all the time. She will quickly tire of each object and will never be satisfied.

It isn't easy for parents to resist the temptation to buy lots of new things for their child. Naturally, they want the best for her. But they need to remember that spoiling their child now will have negative consequences later. It's best to give the little one a few simple toys that have possibilities for engaging her imagination.

Sports help in developing children's motor skills. Not all children are athletic, but all of them enjoy physical activity. Here, too, the possibilities are many and varied. It's best when a father chooses to participate along with his child, both for the sake of developing athletic skills and for the physical contact that both father and child need. Children are delighted beyond measure when they can tumble around on the carpet or the lawn with their father, when they can "rassle him down" and climb all over him. They love to ride on his back like cowboys taming a wild bucking horse. As they grow, they may get excited about playing ball or planning a Saturday bike ride with Dad. Such play strengthens the bond between father and child.

Children of any age, even the very small, love to go swimming with their dad. Water holds a special attraction for most children. And the child who is fearful of water can learn from her father's example and begin to actually enjoy water play.

Long hikes are good for those who have a spirit of adventure. But remember, it's really not much fun for a child to plod for hours along crowded asphalt trails. It's much more interesting to explore a forest or hike up a hill or mountainside where the trails are faint or non-existent. Such an outing can turn into an adventure that children will never forget—especially if Dad can talk about the wildlife of the area, the native plants, the geological features, the Indians who roamed there or the immigrants who settled there.

And then there is the fascinating world of repairs. Think of how many things in one's household need fixing: the vacuum cleaner that's on the blink, the bicycle with a flat tire, the car that needs an oil change. Whenever something needs to be repaired, children should be included in the project.

When a shed needs to be built in the back yard, children can help. Maybe they can put together a little hut of their own, big enough to sleep in.

It's important in all these undertakings to give children tasks that they can carry out all by themselves. If a child is allowed only to hand Dad the hammer or screwdriver, she won't derive much satisfaction from the work. Instead, Dad should assign her responsibility for a specific task that suits her abilities. For example, she could be given a piece of the garden plot; this little strip of land would be her own, so that she can choose seeds, plant them herself, pull weeds and watch her seedlings grow. Such a project is wonderful for a child, allowing her to learn about nature and responsibility at the same time.

Encouraging Questions

There's so much for a child to see, so much to find out! Where does snow come from, Dad? How does water turn into rain? Why are there storms? And trees. Flowers that open. Bees. Fruit that a child can pick and taste. Together, father and child can watch their natural surroundings over the spring months, noticing how new life emerges.

When a child experiences fear during a thunderstorm, it's helpful to have Father near to take her in his arms, or by the hand. He leads her to the window so that they can watch the lightning. She can see that he admires the sky's wild beauty, and he explains electricity to her.

Fathers have a special capacity to promote analytical problem-solving in their children. When a child is faced with a problem she can't solve by herself, she goes to Dad. His response is critical. Does he tell her to go ask Mom? Or does he try to pacify her with superficial comfort—"Don't worry, it'll be okay"? The best response, of course, is to sit down with the child and help her find a way through the problem.

First of all, Dad listens. After the child describes the situation clearly, she and Dad need to think it through and talk it over together—if possible, in a way that allows the child to offer her own ideas. Even if Dad can easily see a solution to the problem, it's often better to help the child discover the solution than simply to present it ready-made. This will stimulate her to think on her own and weigh various alternatives. She learns about causal connections in this way.

If the problem is a broken toy, Dad helps put it together again. If the problem is part of the child's math homework, her father can (most likely) help there as well.

Fathers Are Not Omniscient

The explosion of information today, especially in the area of computer technology, makes it easy for fathers and children to become estranged from each other. Today many fathers feel overwhelmed by what is expected of them. Knowledge is becoming more and more specialized, and none of us can really keep up with it all. A father may be quite competent in his particular field but find that the questions his growing children ask are often beyond his ability to answer. He may reach the point of avoiding his children so as not to reveal his incompetence.

When Dad looks over his child's homework and asks about it, the child may well answer with a wave of her hand, "Oh Dad, you wouldn't understand." This may be threatening to the father who is anxious to maintain his authority. He may manage to make a humorous retort, but still feel so hurt that he decides he needs to demonstrate his superiority in some other realm.

But why shouldn't a father be able to admit that he doesn't know everything? It's better to say in all honesty that he doesn't know than to look for some flimsy excuse that his child can see through anyway. Resorting to pretense and bluffing simply sets up a barrier between father and child.

When a child perceives that her father is completely competent in his line of work and understands his business well, her respect for Dad is not at all diminished when he can't answer a question requiring a different area of expertise. On the contrary, she will respect him even more for being realistic and honest.

Fathers and Schooling

Sadly, many fathers nowadays are so busy that they leave the education of their children entirely up to the schools. Regardless of busyness, parents—especially fathers—still need to take responsibility to supervise the education their children receive.

The influence of schools should not be underestimated. Schools in our day have become independent authorities, so parents should make use of their rights to involve themselves in the education process. They should work closely with their children's teachers. And they should examine the textbooks carefully. If parents visit classes, the teacher will be aware that he or she is accountable to the parents for what their child is being taught.

An important part of guiding a child through school is helping her gain the motivation to work hard. Here again, she needs a model. Her father's attitude toward his job, whether positive or negative, will likely become her own attitude toward schoolwork and other work responsibilities. So if a father wants to see his child succeed in school, he must show the way by example.

Today there is a trend to ignore anything unpleasant and push responsibility onto others rather than accepting it oneself. Given this cultural trend, fathers simply can't expect schools to teach their children a high regard for work. That remains primarily the father's job.

And this goes back to teaching the child about gardening and giving her other tasks at home. Studies have shown that children who have had to take responsibility for animals and plants at an early age are more apt later on to be good caretakers in general and more willing to take on responsibility.

How Does a Father Teach?

First of all, as we have shown, fathers teach by playing. When Dad gathers materials to build something with his child, he won't simply hand the materials to the child, but will get down on the floor or ground next to him and show him some things that can be made with these objects. The child will watch and then try his hand at building the way Daddy does. And when Daddy praises him for his accomplishment, the child is extremely gratified and wants to keep on building more and more things.

But when the child tries to make a structure that won't hold, he knocks it apart in a fit of rage and has no wish to start over. Then Daddy will gently begin building with him again. This is how the little one learns that you don't just give up if something doesn't turn out right on your first try. He learns to try a second time and then a third, even a fourth. And finally he'll succeed. Then he will feel relieved and proud that he saw it through. Such an achievement will have much greater value than any instant success.

An important caution: It's very important to choose playthings that are age-appropriate. The child must be able to develop his skills and abilities as he plays with his toys. They need to be neither too easy nor too difficult for him to master. If building blocks are set in front of a ten-year-old, he will be bored. And if a model airplane is offered to a two-year-old, he won't be able to assemble it, fly it or appreciate it.

The *way* a father teaches has a great influence on children. Research has shown that an authoritarian manner inhibits a child's academic ability.[1] The father who acts like a know-it-all and lords it over his children will soon lose them. Quite simply, the children will no longer have the courage or the incentive to bring their questions to Dad.

It is the father's job to encourage his child—to encourage him, to support him, to find positive things to say. If a father puts his child down by saying, "You ought to know that already!" or "I know you couldn't do it; you can't do anything!" it won't be long before the child will be convinced in his own mind that he _is_ good for nothing. And his life will bear that out, for fathers' words often become self-fulfilling prophecies.

How then should a father teach? As a father and as a friend. Both are important. A father who is merely a pal to his children can't guide them. Only the father who can remain an authority figure, yet still put himself on the child's level, will be able to lead his children to the place where he himself stands. He can show the way to his children.

As we said before, it isn't necessary to be right all the time. In fact, if a father appears to be infallible, his children will feel totally inferior, unable to measure up. Fathers, like anyone else, can be wrong and can make mistakes. So a father needs to be willing to admit his mistake to his child. This will not tarnish the father's image in his child's eyes; on the contrary, he will appear more human and approachable. Then, when the child himself makes a mistake, he's more likely to be honest about it with his dad.

How does a father teach? Most of all through his own behavior, by example, and through the atmosphere he creates. When he is harried, impatient, irritable and nervous, the child cannot open up. But if the father radiates calm, trustworthiness and love, it won't be hard for the child to tackle a new task. For he knows: "My dad won't desert me. He'll catch me if I fall. He is there."

12

THE FATHER AS PRIEST

Showing the Way to God

*I*n some cultures fathers function as priests. They are, so to speak, the connecting link between their families and the world of the gods. The father represents his family to the gods and brings sacrifices on their behalf.

According to Scripture, we are all called to be priests (Ex 19:6; Is 61:6; 1 Pet 2:9). But what does this calling mean for fathers in particular?

Teaching the Faith

The Torah, the Old Testament books of the Law, admonishes fathers again and again: "When your children are old enough to ask . . ." We read in Deuteronomy 6:20-23:

In the future, when your son asks you, "What is the meaning of the stipulations, decrees and laws the LORD our God has commanded you?" tell him: "We were slaves of Pharaoh in Egypt, but the LORD brought us out of Egypt with a mighty hand. Before our eyes the LORD sent miraculous signs and wonders—great and terrible—upon Egypt and Pharaoh and his whole household. But he brought us out from there to bring us in and give us the land that he promised on oath to our forefathers."

In instructing the Israelites about celebrating the Passover, Moses said, "When your children ask you, 'What does this ceremony mean to you?' then tell them, 'It is the Passover sacrifice to the LORD, who passed over the houses of the Israelites in Egypt and spared our homes when he struck down the Egyptians' " (Ex 12:26-27).

"These commandments that I give you today," Moses said later, "are to be upon your hearts. Impress them on your children. Talk about them when you sit at home and when you walk along the road, when you lie down and when you get up" (Deut 6:6-7).

As witnesses of God's intervention, fathers pass on to their children what they themselves have experienced or what has been handed down to them from their own parents and earlier ancestors. This is a key part of their priestly role.

A father's faith must not be abstract; it is history experiened firsthand. As he tells of the great deeds of God, Father awakens in his children a feeling for history as well as an awareness of God. Thus children become involved in global events. They learn to understand the interconnectedness of things. Through his stories a father opens his children's eyes to God's dealings and human actions. In this way history comes alive.

Children need to be prepared to deal with life beyond the family. So Father should help them understand the history of humankind and integrate it into the present. Children should learn to see today in relation to yesterday, the present in relation to the past. In his storytelling a father should also speak of the dangers that lurk in the world, ready to ensnare a person—the secret seducers. Children must learn to recognize the enemy of their souls so that they can be properly forearmed and protected.

Children ask about the past, and their father answers. And one day the children will also ask Father about his own experiences. Then he will tell a story in which he himself plays a part. Later, when the children are older, they will ask their father again—and again he will answer. He will tell about his own experience with God. If this is linked with memories of sin and guilt—memories he would rather forget—he will have an opportunity to talk about forgiveness and grace.

A father is his children's connecting link between the present and the past, and he demonstrates that God is just as present today as in years gone by. A father's testimonies will encourage his children to live their lives in relation to God.

The Praying Father

As a man of God, a father will appeal to God on his children's behalf. In the Old Testament we read how Job brought his children before God in prayer (Job 1:5). This lies at the heart of the father's responsibility. He can represent his children before the face of God and bring their needs to the heavenly Father. He seeks the Lord's counsel and wisdom in all his decisions, and will discuss with God every stage of his children's lives.

There are no hard and fast rules that dictate how a father must exercise his priestly function within his family. For one it may be carried out through holding daily family devotions, while within another family this may not work at all. In general, it seems that when children are still small, it's usually the mother who reads or tells them stories from the Bible, sings with them and then prays with them before they go to sleep. But our experience has shown that children are delighted when Daddy comes to their bedsides too and joins in a prayer to end the day. The children feel surrounded by safety during this prayer time; in fact, they may gladly pray on and on to make these warm moments last as long as possible.

But when prayers or devotions become mere ritual, they lose their power. And sooner or later the children will rebel against participating. Perhaps they don't verbalize their feeling, but they communicate it nonetheless.

I know a family in which devotions had a fixed place in the daily agenda. Every meal ended with verses or even a whole chapter from the Bible, and predictable prayers were repeated day after day, like a talisman intended to protect the children. The parents were faithful in observing this tradition, but there was no joy in it, and no power.

Daily devotions must meet the children's needs. If a family spans a broad age range, it will be especially challenging to find readings that will be helpful for everyone.

Once children grow into adolescence, their father needs to take an increasing role as spiritual leader for them. Otherwise faith may come to be seen as something that is exclusively feminine. Of course Mother can speak just as well about spiritual things, but if she is wise, she will grant her husband many opportunities to exercise spiritual leadership.

The Humble, Honest Father
Naturally, it matters who this father is and what kind of relationship he has with God. If he sees his priestly role merely as a duty he is obligated to carry out, it's better for him to abandon family devotions altogether, lest his children become impatient and cynical and reject the gospel. If he changes the tone of his voice during devotions, uses pious phrases and mouths the same platitudes time after time, he will

lose credibility with his adolescent children. If he speaks to his children of God's love and righteousness and then is harsh and unyielding with his wife, they will notice the discrepancy. No father can inspire his children to love God if he acts like a phony.

Children have a very subtle sensitivity. It's very easy for them to distinguish between pretense and genuineness. So a father who is a leader in the church but fails to practice the fruits of the Spirit within his own family will not be taken seriously.

But if children watch their father in everyday life and see that he is sincere, without hypocrisy, speaking to Mother in the same tone he uses when he speaks to God, then it will be easier for them to accept what he says. If a father is just and merciful in his own house, then he is qualified to speak of the justice and mercy of God. And if his life is marked by love, his children will believe him when he speaks about the love of God.

The most important thing is that the father himself is close to God. That he takes time to appear before the face of God, practicing a genuine prayer life of his own. That he studies the Word, accepts correction, is humble and doesn't try to prove himself infallible to his children.

A father who has the courage to ask his children's forgiveness if he has wronged them will be taken seriously. His inner truth will create such a warm, secure atmosphere that even outsiders will notice that God is present in his household. When that is so, the father need not resort to long speeches about who God is. Even if he doesn't mention God every day, the children see that Dad takes God into account. And they will be drawn quite naturally into a close relationship with God.

They will remember that Dad prayed for a solution to that difficult situation at school—and that God answered in a way that made the problem seem to solve itself.

After a neighbor is seriously injured in a car accident, the children will be aware that Dad has been praying for the neighbor's family for a long time. They will be attentive to his response to the neighbor in this time of need. Perhaps they will join in praying.

And the children are aware that Dad recently experienced a serious setback at work. How will he handle it? If the family is now faced with a difficult decision, they will gather to kneel together and bring the matter before the Lord. Then they will wait with great anticipation to see what God will do and how he will change the situation. They don't know what God will do, but together they trust that he has this situation well in hand.

Fathers have received their priesthood as a holy office from God, and they must allow themselves to be led by God in exercising this office. There are no detailed rules for a father to follow in carrying out this role. But if he is a man of God whose speech and actions are consistent with each other, he will naturally draw his children toward their heavenly Father.

The Father's Image

Father—who is he? How might we draw a picture of him?

He gives his children security, safety and protection. He is a pillar of strength that they can lean on, a fortress.

His word carries weight; for behind a father's word stands his authority. His authority is solid, and that solidity inspires trust. Father's words establish boundaries. They are like walls. His children can lean on them, and within these walls they feel safe. They need these boundaries.

It's natural for children to want complete freedom. They perceive every wall as a restriction. And when they see that others their own age have the freedom to live pretty much as they choose, they may well demand the same freedom of choice. But if their father were to capitulate to such wishes in order to be loved more, or to be regarded by his children's friends as "modern" and "progressive," he wouldn't actually be acting in his children's best interests.

A father must have the courage to be different—to stand by his decisions without looking nervously to the right and the left to see what others are doing and saying. For after all, he makes his decisions based on his responsibility toward his child. He's not simply standing on some rigid principle or tradition, arguing that "we've always done it this way." No, he chooses with his eye on the goal: the mature adult that his child is to become.

Firm boundaries signify *home* for a child. Such walls don't restrict; they protect.

The difference that security makes really depends on what kind of person the father is. It's a matter not only of his strength but also of his truthfulness. His children know they can count on their father, because Father stands by his word. He is dependable, and he is committed to his children. His whole being is honest; nothing is false. Word and being are congruent.

A good father is also able to give comfort. He does so differently from Mother, but every bit as effectively. He can comfort because he understands life and knows all about its difficulties. He's not shocked when a child comes to him with a painful confession. He is able to listen, and when he responds, he means what he says. He is also able to be silent, and he would never do anything to hurt his child deliberately.

When Father is struggling with his own problems, he doesn't allow them to get the better of him. He will still have room in his heart for whatever concerns his child.

He won't spend time nervously polishing up his image so as to look good in his children's eyes. A real father can be short in physical stature without losing any of his greatness. He isn't dependent on the applause of others, because he isn't looking for honor for himself. He would like to serve his children and give them what they need. He wants to be a step ahead of them, able to help them from experience.

He does not insist on being served, making his family wait on him. Instead, he's concerned to see to it that others' needs are met. He will contribute his ideas to improve his workplace and his home community; he'll keep watch over the affairs of his household and be on hand wherever help is needed.

It doesn't matter if his hands are rough from hard work, as long as his eyes look kindly on his children and his hands reach out to hold them. Children will be proud of a father like that.

The Father's Task
The time has come for fathers to return to their families. It is time for families to become places of refuge, not just places to sleep. Families are arteries, the spring from which new life can flow.

Modernization can't be reversed. Every attempt to live as though we were still in an earlier era proves to be unworkable. We are being swept along in history.

Humankind is no longer in control of what it produces. And we have reasons to be fearful of what we ourselves have brought into being. Haven't we already programmed our own destruction? The boldest dreams of the future have proved to be death traps, because people have disregarded God's orders regarding creation. These orders cannot be bent to please us. They are above every trend, every fashion; they are not dependent on the wisdom of the day. They are a divine standard.

But wherever an earthly father acknowledges the rule of the heavenly Father, there is hope. Such a father will say to his children

☐ that there is no justice without God, even when every person believes he or she is doing the right thing;

☐ that without God no peace is possible on this earth, even when peace slogans are echoing around the world;

☐ that without God love is a lie, even when the whole world talks about love;

☐ that without a relationship with the Father in heaven freedom is impossible—even when everyone is talking about the great freedom we can obtain through self-realization;

☐ that only in God can human longings find ultimate fulfillment, because we were made for loving God.

Where a father places himself under God, the family will regain its health. And these healthy families will transform society, inch by inch, so that God's blessing can become visible once again.

13

CARING FOR THE FATHERLESS CHILD

Single Mothers & Father Substitutes

T *his book has mostly been directed toward fathers, inviting them to dis-*
cover their calling. We've tried to make the point that fathers are
crucial for the healthy development of children, and that they can
learn to model God's love for their little ones.

Still, we recognize that there are many families whose father is
absent through either divorce or death. We've already looked at the
difficulties that many of these fatherless children encounter. Is there
any hope for those who are fatherless? What can other adults do to
fill in the gaps?

The Challenge of Single Motherhood
First, let's be realistic about the struggles that face the mother who has

been widowed or divorced. Single motherhood is extremely stressful. The practical issues of supporting the family financially and handling all the household tasks that used to be divided between two people are only the beginning.

The single mother may well face serious disciplinary problems with her children. Social scientists generally acknowledge that children (especially girls) from families with no father behave much more aggressively than children from complete families.[1] This aggression compels the mother to take a resistant stance with her children. And the ensuing duels more often than not end in the child's favor.

Power contests with children are simply more than most mothers can handle. They may reach a point where they no longer know how to cope. The children's aggressiveness elicits an aggressive response from her, but that merely adds fuel to the fire. Such a state of war adds greatly to the mother's already heavy burden.

Added to all this is the inner hurt the mother has suffered through the loss of her husband. Such a wound does not heal quickly; it usually takes a long time to adjust to the new situation. If the marriage ended in divorce, the mother may feel quite bitter—especially if she was not the one who initiated the breakup. This bitterness makes her painfully sensitive, so that she may not be able to take charge of the household. The children sense her weakness immediately. And if they blame their mother for what has happened, her relationship with them becomes even more strained.

The divorced mother is fighting on two fronts at the same time. She hasn't recovered from the emotional turmoil of breaking up with her husband, and she'd like to banish him completely from her life. Yet she continues to catch little glimpses of him in the children, who, after all, carry his genes. So she can never become completely free of him.

She may nurse a desire to punish her ex-husband, yet he is now beyond her reach. So she may try—probably unconsciously—to get revenge on him through the children. Aren't they just like him? The things about her husband that drove her crazy are reflected in his children. Before she realizes it, her anger and disappointment are being directed at them. Usually this is not overt. What may happen is that her reprimands become quite harsh, all out of proportion to the offense. The least resistance causes her to explode.

A single mother tends to be anxious. It used to be that she and her husband handled things together and shared family responsibilities. Now she is forced to make all her decisions alone.

Anxious mothers tend to be overprotective of their children, not allowing them free rein in play for fear they'll get hurt. It's natural for a boy to play rough and test his limits; but now Mom is hovering over her son, trying to rein him in every time he gets a bit rowdy. This is very constraining for the little boy. If his boyish impulses are always being repressed, he becomes insecure and effeminate or else aggressive.

If the mother's anxiety extends to possessiveness, the child's maturation is bound to be hindered. The bond between mother and child may become too strong, blocking the development of the child's ego so that he remains infantile in his behavior. At the same time, aggression is accumulating inside him. This aggression will find expression sooner or later, possibly in depression or psychosomatic disorders.

These are the pitfalls a single mother needs to avoid. So how can she find her way? What can she do to build a new family life in which she and her children can flourish?

Building a New Life

The first task for the newly widowed or divorced mother is to *reorganize family life*. If the mother has lost her husband through death, she may be tempted to deny this painful reality at first and to look to her children for support. The divorced mother's struggle may be similar, but for a different reason. The father is no longer available as a source of support, yet he may be nearby, sometimes dropping in to spend time with the children and sometimes staying away because he is caught up in his new activities and relationships. Such a family is in limbo, unable to reorganize itself and get on with things.

It's crucial, then, for the mother to accept the reality of what has happened. For fatherless children, the mother is the most important stabilizer. Research has shown that if the child is to grow up well-adjusted, the mother's ego strength seems to be even more important than her warmth and tenderness.[2] Security in her sexual identity is important too. Several social scientists have studied single mothers of successful children and discovered that these women had already been relatively secure in their feminine identity before they lost their husbands. So when they had to assume the paternal role in addition to their mothering responsibilities, they succeeded in developing new traits and skills without sacrificing their womanliness.

What should the mother do when she can't come to terms with the new situation? As long as she is caught up in her own pain and problems, she cannot meet her children's needs. She lacks a husband—the fixed pole by which she had always set her course, the mirror in which she recognized herself. She is not protected herself, yet she needs to offer protection to her children. She needs to appear strong, but she is alone. Alone with responsibility, with important decisions, with problems that she thinks she can't handle alone.

The single mother's parents can be of great help at this time, talking through decisions with their daughter and caring for the children when she needs rest. Their role, however, should be mainly to stand beside her in support; they should never usurp her authority or treat her like a child in front of her own children.

The single mother needs to build up a circle of friends outside her family. She may discover other women who find themselves in the same situation. These friends can offer the support and encouragement she needs.

She may want to give in to the temptation to bury herself in her pain, isolating herself as if her life were over. But life goes on. She needs to reconnect with people. This will save her from wallowing in self-pity and living in the past, and it will help her to overcome anxiety and bitterness.

Not only for the mother herself but also for the children, it's very important that the circle of relationships be widened and that their lives be rechanneled. It's time for the family to make plans, to undertake restructuring together, to set new goals.

Assuming that the children are old enough, the mother should consider taking a job outside the home, at least part-time. In the marketplace she can experience a new sense of self-worth and affirmation. And as she begins to feel accepted as a person in her own right, she will find it easier to accept her children and become responsive to her needs.

When the children's father has visitation rights, it can be very hard for the mother, for every time she sees her former husband the old wounds may reopen. Yet the children need to be her primary concern—and for the children's development it is important that the father be included in their lives.

The exception, of course, is when there is danger of abuse. Then it is better to protect the children from their father.

Regardless of the reason for the divorce, the mother should act wisely, carefully considering her children's needs. Even if the father has sinned grievously, it's not helpful for the mother to criticize him regularly to the children. And she should not use them as informers, grilling them after each visit to their father to find out what he is up to. The object, after all, is to restore their trust.

It's crucial for her to realize that *the children are not there to meet her needs; she is there for them.* As she struggles to deal with her turbulent emotions, she should not look to her children for advice and comfort. She needs to look for help outside the family so that she does not lay an adult burden on her children. God, her own loving heavenly Father, is her ultimate resource. She can bring her problems to God, relax in his love and draw on his power.

With God's help, a single mother can succeed in giving her family a new stability. Then her children will have a better chance of recovering from the loss of their father.

The Father Substitute

Countless studies have shown and our own counseling practice has confirmed that fathers are crucial to the healthy development of children—especially boys. If the father is absent because of divorce or death, it's very important that another person, or persons, be there to take his place. A father substitute will never quite replace the birth father, yet he can be of great help as a child grows up.

The idea of a substitute or surrogate father is not new. It even appears in Scripture: Esther had a surrogate father named Mordecai (Esther 2:5-7). Mordecai was an excellent father substitute who made it possible for Esther to realize her potential. He gave direction without restricting. He was there for her, communicating security.

In the Middle Ages, the most respected families in Europe chose father substitutes for their sons. It was common for a boy to be apprenticed at the age of seven, or taken by a trustee who reared him as his own son. Daughters were often sent to relatives to learn housekeeping skills.

Although these practices meant that the children were separated from their biological families, they were accepted into substitute families. To what extent that led to problems we have no way of determining today. We would guess that there were many problems. For example, the children may have felt slighted or neglected, feeling as if their foster parents favored their own children.

Still, today father substitutes are sometimes not an option but a necessity. Who can best play this role?

A father substitute can often be found right within the child's own family. The oldest brother can become a model for the younger ones, or the grandfather may be available to spend time with the children. A teacher or pastor can also take the father's place to a certain extent.

A loving, wise stepfather may be able to help meet the child's needs. Mothers need to realize, however, that a child's relationship with his or her stepfather is sometimes very strained. The child's age may make a difference; younger children are often more likely to accept a stepfather. The stepfather's personality, of course, helps determine whether he can take a major role as a father substitute.

In the case where no male model is available, a woman can take over this job—perhaps the grandmother, or a friend of the family. The important thing is that the child is freed from complete dependence on the mother; his or her horizons will be widened through the influence of someone outside the immediate family.

There are two qualifications for a father substitute: (1) being a good model for the child to emulate and (2) offering safety and security.

Security fosters trust—and if the fatherless child's ability to trust can be protected, he or she will have a much better chance of growing into healthy, whole adulthood.

14

HEALING THE FATHER WOUND

Returning to Our Heavenly Father

*T*here are a few critical questions left to address in this book: What if one's own father failed significantly and has been unwilling to be reconciled to his adult children? How can the wounded son become a good father to his own children?

Is it true that only a secure person can offer security to others? What happens when a father wants to offer security to his children but has never known it himself? And how can he teach his children tolerance and patience when he never experienced these parental qualities in his own childhood? When his own spirit is still wounded from unjust beatings, when he is still deeply hurt by the humiliation he was forced to suffer, how can he teach his own children to forgive?

The wheel cannot turn in reverse, and what has happened cannot be undone. But a new beginning is possible. Our Lord is the source of new life. *And all the negative things that you endured as a child can be transformed into blessing.*

The Power of Forgiveness

I remember one father who felt very sad because he was unable to build good relationships with his children. He could tell that they were avoiding him. They were afraid of him, threatened by his very presence.

"They are relieved when I leave the house," he complained. Then he admitted, "I can't even get along with myself. So how could I expect to get along with my children?"

I asked this man about the relationship he'd had with his own father. And his answer was just what I expected. "My father and I didn't relate well at all. He was too strict and unfair. I always tried to please him. But no matter what I did, it wasn't good enough. He preferred my brother, who was good at everything. I was afraid of my father. He has never loved me. You see, I was conceived unexpectedly. I've never forgiven my father for not accepting me."

Because the son didn't get along with his father, he had looked to his mother for comfort. As he grew up, he tried homosexuality. It took years before he was able to redirect his feelings and desires toward women. Even then, it seemed as though his life was doomed to failure. The destructive hatred kept gnawing at him inside. Having become severely depressed, he had come to me for help.

Somewhere inside this man there still existed the hurting child who was unable to forget his injury. The image of the father-as-enemy had etched itself so deeply into his soul that it was still affecting him and everything he did. It had become a kind of pattern that subconsciously dictated his behavior. Because of his hostility toward his father, he was not free to relate lovingly toward his children. Without realizing it, he had become just as harsh and antagonistic as his own father. The result was that his children rejected him.

As long as he persisted in carrying around the unprocessed burden of his own father-son problem, he would be unable to respond to his children's needs. A process of inner healing needed to begin. He needed to consciously confront his bitterness and begin to forgive his father instead of blaming him over and over.

Naturally, he thought this would be impossible. Hatred had eaten too deeply into his being.

Shortly after our first conversation, his aged father became very ill. The son refused to see him; he wanted to banish his father from his life altogether. But then the unexpected happened. In his helplessness, the old man began to read the Bible. Then he called his son and asked for forgiveness. A reconciliation followed—and new seed was sown.

Giving Our Memories to God

Even when we have suffered grievous hurts and the injustice cuts deep, new seed can be sown in our hearts. But before that can happen, the old memories must be released. This is a matter of one's will—not of one's feelings.

If I wish to become a better father but am still held prisoner by my unhappy past, healing will come through prayer. Through a process of prayer, I can revisit all the stages of my life and express to God all the disappointments and bitter memories that come to mind. This conscious verbalization is a kind of severing. One scene after another, one cruel word after another, I give to God.

Then, no matter how often my memory tries to recall these thoughts, I refuse to entertain them. I refuse to relive the past, to taste the old bitterness even one more time. I tell myself, "I will no longer be party to that inner rehashing of wrongs, that secret self-pity. Those things don't concern me anymore." Even if these thoughts arise a thousand times to demand retribution and vengeance, I resolve to defeat them a thousand times, until the power of the negative is broken.

What about this person who has brought so much hardship and pain into my life—my father?

Did God not use this man to give me life? Wasn't he the tool that God's hand used to shape me? So I now place this tool back in God's hands, without bitterness. For God is greater than I. He knows what to do with my father.

I look to God and forget what lies behind me, reach forward toward what lies ahead (Phil 3:13). I will not let old pain hold me back. Why should I allow myself to be enslaved any longer? I am free. Jesus has redeemed me through his cross, and I have given everything back to God.

And everything that God takes in his hands he will transform. He will change my pain into blessing—a blessing that will also affect my family. The word from the prophet Isaiah holds true for each of us, even when we feel hopeless:

Forget the former things;
> do not dwell on the past.

See, I am doing a new thing!
> Now it springs up; do you not perceive it?

I am making a way in the desert
> and streams in the wasteland. (Is 43:18-19)

Earthly Fathers, Heavenly Father

I know people who cannot call God Father. In fact, anytime someone speaks of God, these people shrink back. When they are invited to join in praying the Lord's Prayer—which begins, "Our Father in heaven"—they cannot utter a word.

Father was the one who hurt them so deeply, who criticized them, abused them, treated them unfairly, abandoned them. And they are not yet free of the suffering he caused. This father, who abused his daughter sexually, was supposed to reflect the heavenly Father, who looks upon his child with eyes of purest love. And this father who always humiliated his son, so that the boy experienced one failure after another as he grew up because he subconsciously needed to meet his dad's expectations—how can such a father image reflect the true Father?

If a woman's own father treated her brutally, how can she believe that God is merciful? If a boy was forced to witness injustice day after day, how can he grow up trusting that God is just? Can he have faith in a Father full of goodness, when his own father was arbitrary, unpredictable or indifferent?

The mistrust that a child learns through being disappointed in his or her father will later be transferred to God. Such a person will experience God as threatening.

Can a broken, distorted father image still reflect goodness, mercy, kindness, love, truth and faithfulness? Isn't it more like a crazy-house mirror, making God look like a monster just waiting for a child to approach him trustingly so that he can smash this little one to the ground? Perhaps God is busy thinking up horrible tortures for this child, just for his own amusement.

Show Us the Father

"I have heard that God is love," you may say. "I really want to believe that, but my heart is afraid."

Who is the heavenly Father? Where is he—the Father who embraces his child in love, accepts his child selflessly, protects and carries his child? How can we find the Father who, like a loving gardener, gives his child space to unfold like a tender young plant?

Every human being yearns to encounter this Father. This yearning drives countless young men and women to wander from one continent to another, hoping to find the Father-love that will give their lives meaning. This is the yearning of people who gather around a leader who promises to meet all their needs. The longing of those who try to forget their disappointment through a chemical high.

Where is the Father who can satisfy the longing of all people? The Father who hears and answers when his child calls—and whose answer the child can count on?

"Lord, show us the Father!" begged the apostle Philip.

And Jesus answered, "Don't you know me, Philip, even after I have been among you such a long time?" (Jn 14:8-9).

Can it be that the Father has been in our midst for a very long time, though we have not recognized him? That he has been here, waiting for us, while we were crying out for him?

Perhaps we've been like Mary, who did not recognize the risen Christ. Mired in her pain, enveloped in mourning, she believed he was the gardener—until Jesus spoke to her, calling her by name: "Mary!" (Jn 20:10-16).

And the two disappointed men on the road to Emmaus didn't recognize Jesus either, because their minds were occupied with nothing but negative memories. But Jesus explained the Scriptures to them, and their eyes began to be opened. And when he sat down with them and broke bread, they saw him for who he was (Lk 24:13-35).

Just as the eyes of the disciples in New Testament times had to be opened, so God must open our eyes today so that we can see the Father: the Father's goodness, his incomprehensible mercy and his inexhaustible love.

The Way to the Father

"Anyone who has seen me has seen the Father," Jesus announced (Jn 14:9). So whoever wants to know the Father must meet Jesus first. For "no one comes to the Father except through me," Jesus says.

He is the way to the Father (Jn 14:6).

Jesus' whole life was wrapped up in listening to the heavenly Father and revealing the Father's heart. Even at the age of twelve, Jesus found the Father irresistibly fascinating; already he knew that he felt at home only when he was in his Father's presence (Lk 2:41-49). His Father's presence was not restricting; it was liberating—because there was a deep relationship of trust between Father and Son. Just as the Father knew the Son, the Son also knew the Father (Jn 10:15).

So the Son knew that he could rely on his Father—that the Father would not desert him (Jn 8:29). There was such a remarkable oneness between Father and Son that Jesus could say, "I and the Father are one" (Jn 10:30), and "All that belongs to the Father is mine" (Jn 16:15). This union was grounded in love and found its expression in mutual honor (Jn 8:49). The Son's wish to do the Father's will was the substance of his life; it was his very food (Jn 4:34). And so Father God was able to point to Jesus and call him "my Son, whom I love" (Mt 3:17).

Jesus' dependence on his Father was so absolute that he could do nothing on his own; he did only what he saw his Father doing (Jn 5:19). Yet this was no restriction of freedom, but rather a prerequisite for the creative power of love.

A power without weakness. A love without shadow. It was this love that constrained the Son to do the Father's will. And thus the Father's being is mirrored in the Son.

When we read Jesus' words to the needy people who surrounded him, we hear echoes of the Father's words: "Therefore my heart yearns for him; I have great compassion for him" (Jer 31:20). This Father knows what his children need (Mt 6:8). Even when we are unfaithful, he remains faithful (2 Tim 2:13). For our heavenly Father loves us (Jn 16:27).

Jesus wants to bring you into this relationship with the Father, so that you may see into the Father-heart of God and not be afraid any longer (Mt 10:29-31; 28:10; Jn 20:19).

The Father's Mirror

You see, it would be wrong to direct all the yearning of our hearts toward our earthly fathers. Ultimately this man who is my father cannot show me the heavenly Father. And it's at this point that Jesus enters my field of vision.

God, who is invisible Spirit, created earthly fathers to represent the father role in a visible way. By means of the earthly father, each child was supposed to see what God is like, so that each of us could come into a trusting relationship with our divine Father. We were meant to take delight in the father-child relationship.

But through human disobedience, a rift developed. The connection between the eternal Father and the earthly father was destroyed, so that men could no longer reflect the character of God to their children. Instead, the enemy usurped God's place, darkened the father image and distorted it into such a horrible picture that Jesus said, "You belong to your father, the devil" (Jn 8:44).

Still, the everlasting Father's mercy was greater. In Jesus, God gives himself to us in a way we can recognize. His goodness, his patience, his mercy—all of this becomes visible in the life of Jesus. His justice, which is so different from our concept of justice. His power, which conquers even death. Full of compassion, he heals the brokenhearted and binds up their wounds (Ps 147:3).

In Jesus God gives us a whole and undimmed father image. Whoever sees Jesus will recognize the Father.

Returning to the Father

Jesus' whole life shows us who the Father is, but he also told a story that illuminates his Father's character: the parable of the prodigal son (Lk 15:11-32). Perhaps a better name for it would be "the parable of the rediscovered Father." This story uses no theological phrases; its language is so simple that anyone can understand it.

It begins with a father who is loving and generous. He is also wise, for he is willing to release his younger son when the young man expresses the wish to be free. If he had denied his son's urge toward freedom, the son would have resented the father forever.

The son felt restricted by his life at home, limited in his options. Everything in the world beyond seemed enticing. Life with Father had lost its charm. So, equipped with his early inheritance, he rushed headlong into freedom—and ended up imprisoned.

Having gambled away all his hopes and hit rock bottom, he suddenly had a vision of his father's face. For the first time, he saw not just *what* he had given up but *whom* he had given up. He had had everything he needed, *because he had a father who loved him.*

So the son began to draw comparisons. Everyone he had met in the world wanted something from him. And once he had nothing more to give to his so-called friends, they had lost all interest in him. In fact, no one was interested in him anymore—except his father. For the old man loved his son, simply because he was his son, a son whom no one could replace.

What everyone called a "good time" had once seemed very attractive. But now it sickened the young man. Once the glamour was stripped away, the "good time" was revealed as a voracious monster whose appetite was insatiable.

The son had absolutely nothing left—except his father. And the more he thought about his father, the more he longed to see him again. And finally he had only one desire: to return to his father.

But how? Just as he was—a loser, a failure?

He had gambled away everything his father had given him. Nothing remained except his disappointment in himself. The awareness of having failed. Guilt over the lost years had burned deep into his soul, leaving painful wounds.

There was only one person who could heal wounds like these: his father. No one could comfort as he could.

So the young man set off to his father's house. In his lostness he had learned to know himself. There was nothing attractive left, nothing left for him to be proud of. All his dreams had been shattered, and even his ragged clothes stank of the pigsty.

The father saw him approaching in the distance and ran down the road to meet him. But even wrapped in his father's embrace, the son knew that he could not presume on his rights as a son. He had thrown those rights away.

Yet his father was still his father. The old man did not humiliate his son further by saying, "I knew all along that your great plans would fail." He offered not a word of reproach or accusation—only love. A love that was eager to give.

In his father's arms the young man realized what it meant to be the son of this man—a father who was ready to forgive and accept, as if there had been no separation at all.

And once the son had looked into his father's heart, it would never occur to him to rebel a second time. For what he had resisted in his youth was *his own image of his father*. And now he knew that this image had not reflected the true nature of his father.

As Jesus painted this picture of his heavenly Father, the disciples recognized that God is a loving, tender Father. That God had been waiting for them to return to his embrace.

And the earthly father, who for his part learns to identify with Jesus, can at last convey to his child this secret, the shining face of God. The hearts of fathers can be made new and can be opened up to their sons and daughters, so that a people will be prepared for the great day of revelation, when the love of our heavenly Father will blaze forth and make the whole world new.

Notes

Introduction

[1]Peter Härtling, *Der Vater*, ed. Johannes Glötzner (Frankfurt am Main: Fischer Taschenbuch Verlag, 1983), p. 22. The translation is our own.

Chapter 1: Images of Father in Our World

[1]H. B. Biller, "The Father and Sex Role Development," in *The Role of the Father in Child Development*, ed. M. Lamb, 2nd ed. (New York: John Wiley & Sons, 1981), p. 333.

Chapter 2: Fatherhood Across Cultures

[1]The examples in this section are drawn from M. M. Katz and M. I. Konner, "The Role of the Father: An Anthropological Perspective," in *The Role of the Father in Child Development*, ed. M. Lamb, 2nd ed. (New York: John Wiley & Sons, 1981), pp. 155-81.

[2]Quoted in W. A. Visser't Hooft, *Gottes Vaterschaft im Zeitalter der Emanzipation* (Frankfurt am Main: Ev. Verlagswerk, Verlag Josef Knecht, 1982), p. 45.

[3]G. R. Leslie and S. K. Korman, *The Family in Social Context*, 6th ed. (New York: Oxford University Press, 1985), pp. 114-21.

[4]*The Works of Hsüntze* (London: Arthur Probsthain, 1928), p. 307.

[5]Leslie and Korman, *The Family in Social Context*, pp. 79-107.

Chapter 3: The Father in Western Europe & North America

[1]G. R. Leslie and S. K. Korman, *The Family in Social Context*, 6th ed. (New York: Oxford University Press, 1985), pp. 121-27.

[2]Ibid., pp. 149-53.

[3]Ibid., pp. 153-58.

[4]*The Histories of Polybius,* ed. W. R. Paton (Cambridge, Mass.: Harvard University Press, 1923), p. 285.

[5]Quoted in W. A. Visser't Hooft, *Gottes Vaterschaft im Zeitalter der Emanzipation* (Frankfurt am Main: Ev. Verlagswerk, Verlag Josef Knecht, 1982), p. 107.

Chapter 4: Revolt & Emancipation

[1]Friedrich Nietzsche, *Twilight of the Idols and The Anti-Christ* (New York: Penguin, 1895), pp. 158, 169.

[2]Albert Einstein, *Ideas and Opinions* (New York: Crown, 1954), p. 48.

[3]Paul M. van Buren, *The Secular Meaning of the Gospel* (New York: Macmillan, 1960), p. 103.

[4]Plato *The Republic* 562. D—563. A, quoted in *The Conflict of Generations in Ancient Greece and Rome,* ed. Stephen Bertman (Amsterdam: B. R. Grüner, 1976), p. 42.

[5]W. A. Visser't Hooft, *Gottes Vaterschaft im Zeitalter der Emanzipation* (Frankfurt am Main: Ev. Verlagswerk, Verlag Josef Knecht, 1982), pp. 133-35.

[6]Ibid., p. 84.

[7]H. Ebeling, *Die Reise in die Vergangenheit* (Braunschweig, Germany: Georg Westermann, 1972), 4:215.

Chapter 5: The Cost of Fatherlessness

[1]H. B. Biller, "Father Absence, Divorce and Personality Development," in *The Role of the Father in Child Development,* ed. M. Lamb, 2nd ed. (New York: John Wiley & Sons, 1981), pp. 489-552.

[2]J. Wallerstein and J. Kelly, "Children and Divorce: A Review," *Social Work,* November 1979, pp. 468-75.

[3]H. B. Biller, *Paternal Deprivation: Family, School, Sexuality and Society* (Lexington, Mass.: Heath, 1974), cited in Biller, "Father Absence, Divorce and Personality Development," p. 521.

[4]N. D. Brill and E. H. Listen, "Paternal Loss," in *Adults with Emotional Disorders,* Archives of General Psychiatry 14 (1966), pp. 307-14.

[5]A. D. Hart, *Children and Divorce* (Waco, Tex.: Word Books, 1982), pp. 15-16.

[6]Michael E. Lamb, "Fathers and Child Development," in *The Role of the Father in Child Development,* ed. M. Lamb, 2nd ed. (New York: John Wiley & Sons, 1981), p. 28.

Chapter 6: Effects of Fatherlessness

[1]H. B. Biller, "The Father and Sex Role Development," in *The Role of the Father in Child Development,* ed. M. Lamb, 2nd ed. (New York: John Wiley & Sons, 1981), p. 323. Also G. J. M. Aardweg, *Das Drama des gewöhnlichen Homosexuellen* (Neuhausen-Stuttgart:

Hänssler Verlag, 1985), pp. 207-11.

[2]J. Money and A. Ehrhardt, *Man and Woman, Boy and Girl* (Baltimore, Md.: Johns Hopkins University Press, 1972), cited in H. B. Biller, "Father Absence, Divorce and Personality Development," in *The Role of the Father in Child Development*, ed. M. Lamb, 2nd ed. (New York: John Wiley & Sons, 1981), p. 496.

[3]G. A. Rekers, *Shaping Your Child's Sexual Identity* (Grand Rapids, Mich.: Baker Book House, 1982), pp. 129-39.

[4]G. Jacobsen and R. G. Ryder, "Parental Loss and Some Characteristics of the Early Marriage Relationship," *American Journal of Orthopsychiatry* 39 (1969): 779-87.

[5]Biller, "Father Absence, Divorce and Personality Development," p. 495.

[6]Rekers, *Shaping Your Child's Sexual Identity*, pp. 30-31.

[7]Biller, "Father Absence, Divorce and Personality Development," pp. 523-27.

[8]N. Radin, "The Role of the Father in Cognitive, Academic and Intellectual Development," in *The Role of the Father in Child Development*, ed. M. Lamb, 2nd ed. (New York: John Wiley & Sons, 1981), pp. 394, 402.

[9]W. Mischel, "Father Absence and Delay of Gratification," *Journal of Abnormal and Social Psychology* 62 (1962): 116-24.

[10]Biller, "Father Absence, Divorce and Personality Development," p. 517.

[11]Ibid., p. 518.

[12]J. A. M. Meerloo, "The Father Cut the Cord: The Rise of the Father as Initial Transparence Figure," *American Journal of Psychotherapy* 10 (1956): 471-80.

[13]Cited in A. Clarke-Stewart, S. Friedmann and I. Koch, *Child Development* (New York: John Wiley & Sons, 1985), p. 86.

Chapter 7: Healthy Marriage

[1]R. D. Parke and B. R. Tinsley, "The Father's Role in Infancy: Determinants of Involvement in Caregiving," in *The Role of the Father in Child Development*, ed. M. Lamb, 2nd ed. (New York: John Wiley & Sons, 1981), p. 443.

Chapter 8: The Father as Role Model

[1]Erik Erikson, *Childhood and Society*, 2nd ed. (New York: W. W. Norton, 1963), p. 147.

[2]Cited in V. J. Maechtlinger, "The Father in Psychoanalytic Theory," in *The Role of the Father in Child Development*, ed. M. Lamb, 2nd ed. (New York: John Wiley & Sons, 1981), pp. 121-29.

Chapter 9: The Father as Disciplinarian

[1]Frank A. Pedersen, "Father Influences Viewed in a Family Context," in *The Role of the Father in Child Development*, ed. M. Lamb, 2nd ed. (New York: John Wiley & Sons, 1981), p. 298.

[2]Jean Piaget, cited in A. Clarke-Stewart, S. Friedman and I. Koch, *Child Development* (New York: John Wiley & Sons, 1985), pp. 543-45.

[3]Lawrence Kohlberg, cited in T. Lickona, *Moral Development and Behavior* (New York: Holt, Rinehart & Winston, 1976), pp. 31-53.

Chapter 10: The Father as a Man

[1]P. S. Sears, "Child-Rearing Factors Related to Playing of Sex-Typed Roles," *American Psychologist* 8 (1953): 431.

Chapter 11: The Father as Teacher

[1]N. Radin, "Role of the Father in Cognitive, Academic and Intellectual Development," in *The Role of the Father in Child Development*, ed. M. Lamb, 2nd ed. (New York: John Wiley & Sons, 1981), p. 391.

Chapter 13: Caring for the Fatherless Child

[1]H. B. Biller, "Father Absence, Divorce and Personality Development," in *The Role of the Father in Child Development*, ed. M. Lamb, 2nd ed. (New York: John Wiley & Sons, 1981), p. 503.

[2]Ibid., p. 532.